Founded in 1807, John Wiley & Sons is the oldest independent publishing company in the United States. With offices in North America, Europe, Australia, and Asia, Wiley is globally committed to developing and marketing print and electronic products and services for our customers' professional and personal knowledge and understanding.

The Wiley Finance series contains books written specifically for finance and investment professionals as well as sophisticated individual investors and their financial advisors. Book topics range from portfolio management to e-commerce, risk management, financial engineering, valuation and financial instrument analysis, as well as much more.

For a list of available titles, visit our Web site at www.WileyFinance.com.

Evaluating Hedge Fund and CTA Performance

Data Envelopment Analysis Approach

GREG N. GREGORIOU
JOE ZHU

John Wiley & Sons, Inc.

To Alec and Yao—J.Z.

In loving memory of my father Nicholas
and my mother Evangelia—G.N.G.

Published by John Wiley & Sons, Inc., Hoboken, New Jersey.
Published simultaneously in Canada.

For general information about our other products and services, please contact our Customer Care Department within the United States at 800-762-2974, outside the United States at 317-572-3993 or fax 317-572-4002.

Wiley also publishes its books in a variety of electronic formats. Some content that appears in print may not be available in electronic books. For more information about Wiley products, visit our web site at www.wiley.com.

Library of Congress Cataloging-in-Publication Data:

Gregoriou, Greg N., 1956–
    Evaluating hedge fund and CTA performance : data envelopment analysis approach / Greg N. Gregoriou, Joe Zhu.
      p. cm. — (Wiley finance series)
    Includes index.
    ISBN-13 978-0-471-68185-4 (cloth/cd-rom)
    ISBN-10 0-471-68185-7 (cloth/cd-rom)
  1. Hedge funds—Evaluation.   2. Data envelopment analysis.   I. Zhu, Joe, 1968– II. Title. III. Series.
    HG4530.G73 2005
    332.64'5—dc22

                                 2004028303

Printed in the United States of America

10 9 8 7 6 5 4 3 2 1

Contents

Preface

The growth of hedge funds and managed futures over the last few years has been fueled by the volatile market environment. Using dynamic strategies hedge funds and managed futures can diversify, reduce volatility, and enhance portfolio returns. Hedge funds have experienced a dramatic rate of growth as a result of past bear markets. With many pension funds, endowment funds, fund of hedge fund managers, high–net worth individuals, and institutional investors scrambling for downside protection in down markets, this alternative class has become the darling of the investment industry. Because of their low and even negative correlation to traditional stock and bond market indices, hedge funds and commodity trading advisors (CTAs) can offer a safe haven.

However, selecting hedge funds, funds of hedge funds (FOFs), and CTAs is not that easy. The numbers involved—approximately 6,500 hedge funds, 700 FOFs, and 500 CTAs—further complicate the manager selection process. Due to the cumbersome passive and active benchmarks traditionally used to evaluate the nonnormal returns of hedge funds and CTAs, better models are required to examine their performance. As an alternative and complementary performance measure, data envelopment analysis (DEA) adds further insight by accurately measuring the efficiency/performance of hedge funds, funds of hedge funds, and CTAs. It further provides a competitive advantage in highlighting efficient funds subject to their input and output criteria. By simply using multiple inputs and multiple outputs, funds are compared against each other, producing efficiency scores. It is with these efficiency scores that investors can compare and contrast their choice of hedge fund managers and CTAs. We believe that DEA will become a widely used technique to screen and assess hedge fund manager and CTA selection.

Acknowledgments

The authors would like to thank Professor Thomas Schneeweis at the Isenberg School of Management/University of Massachusetts and Director/Editor of the Centre for International Securities and Derivatives Markets (CISDM)/Journal of Alternative Investments (JAI) for supplying the hedge fund and CTA databases. We also thank Raj Gupta, Research Director/Assistant Editor of CISDM/JAI and Dr. Ellen Yan, Executive Director at CISDM for her assistance and help with questions regarding the data.

We would like to thank Strategic Financial Solutions LLC, creators of the PerTrac Analytical Platform (www.pertrac.com), an asset allocation and investment analysis software. PerTrac and their representative Tate Haymond proved instrumental in the research process. Data were calculated with PerTrac and then exported into the *DEAFrontier Basic* to achieve the efficiency scores using the various models. Definitions for inputs and outputs were reproduced from the PerTrac Manual 2004.

We also thank Richard E. Oberuc president of Burlington Hall Asset Management and chairman of the Foundation for Managed Derivatives Research who developed the LaPorte Asset Allocation System (www.laportesoft.com). The Sharpe ratios and ending millions managed were obtained using the LaPorte investment analysis software. Mr. Oberuc was also helpful in the research process.

We thank Associate Professor of Finance Bing Liang in the Department of Finance and Operations Management at the University of Massachusetts at Amherst, Isenberg School of Management for reviewing the Introduction and Fund Selection sections of Chapter 1. We also thank Fabrice Rouah, PhD (Candidate) in finance in the Faculty of Management at McGill University, Montreal, Canada for helpful comments.

We finally thank Bill Falloon senior finance editor for his great support and comments, Alexia Meyers the production editor for meticulously working on the manuscript, and Karen Ludke—all of John Wiley and Sons. We would also like to thank Fine Composition, and in particular Joanna V. Pomeranz for her excellent work on this project.

CHAPTER 1

Fund Selection and Data Envelopment Analysis

INTRODUCTION

Since Alfred Winslow Jones created the first hedge fund in 1949, the hedge fund universe has grown to comprise nearly 7,000 funds, in addition to approximately 750 funds of hedge funds (baskets of hedge funds). The popularity of alternative assets like hedge funds and managed futures can be explained by their diversification capacity, which investors have become especially interested in since the market crash of October 1987. Because of their low or even negative correlation to stock and bond markets, hedge funds and managed futures are considered the best instruments for protecting investor capital while providing absolute returns (Schneeweis and Spurgin, 1998).

The lackluster performance of traditional asset classes over the last few years has encouraged many high–net worth individuals, pension funds, companies, investment banks, and endowments to commit more to alternative investments to improve overall returns and simultaneously reduce risk exposure during increased market turmoil. This emerging investment arena can also provide entrance to the more dynamic and lucrative global futures markets.

Hedge funds and managed futures differ from asset classes such as mutual funds because they are not affected by market movements. This is important for investors, because *the risk of a particular investment can be reduced and performance increased by combining uncorrelated securities in various asset classes* (Markowitz, 1952). Most hedge funds are limited to a maximum of 100 investors and are unregulated by the Securities Exchange Commission (SEC) because they are directed to sophisticated and high–net worth investors. Hedge funds can assume both long and short positions and buy undervalued and short overvalued securities in virtually any stock market. There are approximately a dozen various hedge fund strategies and a handful of managed futures classifications, each of which provides varying levels of return and risk, but all aim to reduce volatility in turbulent markets while delivering absolute returns under any market conditions.

However, performance measurement of hedge funds that use standard market indices as benchmarks has been problematic, since their very nature is alien to that of stock and bond funds. Hedge funds have nonlinear returns due to long/short positions, derivatives, and option-like fee contracts resulting in significant skewness and kurtosis (Agarwal and Naik, 2004; Fung and Hsieh, 1997, 1999; Liang, 2003). So the inclusion of hedge funds in investor portfolios calls for appraisal methodologies that are appropriate for handling the asymmetrical returns they produce. This is even more important given that hedge fund manager selection is a precise process for appraising both risk and reward.

Some benchmarks may be easier for hedge fund managers and commodity trading advisors (CTAs) to outperform because of the large number of funds making up the indices; this provides managers with an opportunity to add value (Wander, 2003, p. 54). Hedge funds and CTAs can outperform traditional long-only indices because they make use of dynamic trading strategies, derivatives strategies, short selling, and leverage to magnify returns.

The growth of CTAs has somewhat mirrored the growth of hedge funds. A CTA is a person or a firm that buys or sells commodity futures or options contracts for profit on various world markets. CTAs also provide advice indirectly to others on these activities. CTAs must be registered with the Commodity Futures Trading Commission (CFTC), and are required to adhere to disclosure and reporting rules and to maintain appropriate records. CTAs trade a variety of futures and indices, with the main areas consisting of currencies, commodities, equities, and fixed income.

CTAs now manage approximately $120 billion. The majority are trend-followers, and generate earnings by identifying trends in global markets. They use proprietary trading systems and generally experience lower maximum drawdowns in negative S&P 500 months and in extreme negative market events than the average equity mutual fund (Gregoriou and Rouah 2004).

Edwards and Caglayan (2001) note that CTAs tend to outperform hedge funds in bear markets and underperform them in bull markets. They achieve this through the use of strategies and derivative instruments such as short-selling, options, and futures, coupled with leverage to magnify returns. Several academic studies have argued that the optimal allocation of hedge funds and/or CTAs in traditional stock and bond portfolios should be approximately 10 to 20% (Karavas, 2000; Kat, 2004; Popova et al., 2003; Cvitanic et al., 2002). With this in mind, sophisticated investors and pension funds are slowly increasing their exposure to alternative investments from 5% to 10–15% for downside equity risk management (Schneeweis, Spurgin, and Potter 1996; Capocci and Hübner, 2003).

According to a recent report by the Barclay Trading Group (2003), managed futures grew by nearly 30% during 2003. An older report by JP Morgan (1994) concludes that allocating 15% or more to managed futures in traditional stock and bond investment portfolios would significantly reduce risk and increase return. In addition, a Chicago Mercantile Exchange study (1999) concluded that portfolios containing 20% managed futures yield up to 50% more returns with the same amount of risk than stock and bond portfolios. The Chicago Board of Trade (2003) concluded that a portfolio with the greatest returns and the least amount of risk consisted of 45% stocks, 35% bonds, and 20% managed futures. Including managed futures in traditional stock and bond portfolios creates an effect of diminishing the standard deviation at a faster rate than hedge funds can, without the unwanted symptoms of skewness and kurtosis as stated by Kat (2004, p. 5). However, it is important to keep in mind when adding hedge funds to traditional investment portfolios that they are likely to increase kurtosis and negative skewness because of the abnormality of their returns (Fung and Hsieh, 1997): the main drawback of this alternative asset class. Hedge funds also display fat tails, which reflects a greater number of extreme events than one would normally anticipate (Fung and Hsieh, 2000).

This book compares hedge fund and CTA performance using the alternative measure of Data Envelopment Analysis (DEA). DEA is a versatile method that uses multiple inputs and multiple outputs to assess hedge fund and CTA returns, thereby avoiding the problems inherent in using traditional passive and active benchmarks. DEA lends itself naturally to assessing the relative performance of hedge funds by making it possible to measure a hedge fund's efficiency relative to the best-performing hedge fund. This allows us to identify the driving factors that determine the efficiency of hedge funds, funds of hedge funds, and CTAs.

With the recent rise in studies investigating hedge fund (Capocci and Hübner, 2003) and CTA performance (Kat, 2004; Martellini and Vaissié, 2004; Hübner and Papageorgiou, 2004; Capocci, 2004), DEA is the perfect complementary technique to examine the efficiency of fund manager selection. Furthermore, the various DEA models used throughout this book can be used as guides for investors to examine potential funds for their portfolios.

FUND SELECTION

The process of identifying the best hedge fund managers through complex research is an art. Manager selection, or due diligence, is based on the fact that superior hedge fund managers can be identified because they generally display good stock selection abilities under a variety of different economic conditions (Gregoriou, Rouah, and Sedzro, 2002; Anson, 2000). However, the selection process requires assessment of both qualitative and quantitative characteristics. It is important to note that investment in alternative asset classes can greatly enhance returns, but if the manager selection process is performed incorrectly, these returns are likely to be mitigated.

Performance measurement is an important piece of the process that should not be neglected. The use of mean-variance portfolio analysis using computer spreadsheet optimizers is widespread, but there are many problems with such numerical algorithms. Selecting and constructing a fund of hedge funds is difficult. However, we find that by simply using user-friendly menus to obtain various statistics, it is possible to create a simulated FOF or even a group of CTAs with high historical returns, low volatility, and low correlation to the markets.

As noted, comparing hedge funds and CTAs to the various passive or active indices may result in incorrect performance assessment. Their dynamic nature makes comparison with passive long-only and active benchmarks problematic. The hedge fund manager and CTA selection process is actually more complex than it appears because of the nonnormality of hedge fund and CTA returns. Although many studies have used the S&P 500 and other static market indices to examine hedge fund and CTA classifications, the results obtained may not be accurate (Gregoriou, Rouah, and Sedzro, 2002; Edwards and Caglayan, 2001).

A passive futures index is based on a buy-and-hold strategy that maintains long-only commodity investments; it cannot be used, however, as a benchmark for strategies that hold short positions or trade financial futures contracts (Schneeweis and Spurgin, 1997, p. 33). An active index tracks the dynamic strategies using a 12-month moving average trading rule encompassing 25 actively traded commodity and financial futures contracts (Schneeweis, Spurgin, and Georgiev, 2001, p. 3). Some active indices such as the Mount Lucas Management Index (MLM) provides a partial explanation of CTA returns; however, the tracking error between the MLM index and CTAs is considered quite sizeable (Schneeweis and Spurgin, 1997, p. 34). Both passive and active managed futures indices are not free from tracking error, and selecting appropriate benchmarks to evaluate CTAs is difficult (Schneeweis and Spurgin, 1997). The authors further suggest that CTA based indices may be the best option as benchmarks; however, month-to-month comparisons of the index returns display large inconsistency in some months.

With only traditional passive and active benchmarks, how can an investor or a FOF manager compare the performance of a hedge fund or a CTA? Recent studies have used active hedge fund and CTA indices, but the problem is compounded because the individual hedge fund and CTA indices are not really typical for each classification (Chatiras, 2004, pp. 1–2).

Several authors have also used multifactor models to examine hedge fund and CTA performance (Edwards and Caglayan, 2000; Schneeweis and Spurgin, 1997). Due to their nonnormal characteristics, it is difficult to find appropriate active benchmarks, and in some cases the use of traditional benchmarks has resulted in low *R*-squared values because hedge funds do not have stable exposure to market factors over time (Brealey and Kaplanis, 2001). Furthermore, hedge funds are absolute return vehicles. Their primary aim is to provide superior performance with low volatility in both bull and bear markets. More sophisticated appraisal techniques, such as data envelopment analysis (DEA), are needed.

DEA yields many advantages over traditional parametric techniques, because regression analysis approximates the efficiency of hedge funds and CTAs under investigation relative to the average performance. DEA can play an important and primordial role in hedge fund manager and CTA selection because it eliminates the cumbersome benchmark selection process and the need to use linear factor models, such as the Capital Asset Pricing Model.

WHAT IS DATA ENVELOPMENT ANALYSIS?

Data envelopment analysis (DEA) is a data-oriented approach for evaluating the performance of a set of peer entities called Decision making units (DMUs) whose performance is characterized by multiple measures/indicators. The definition of a DMU is generic and flexible. In our case, DMU refers to a CTA or a hedge fund. As noted in Cooper, Seiford, and Zhu (2004), recent years have seen a great variety of applications of DEA for use in evaluating the performances of many different kinds of entities engaged in many different activities in many different contexts in many different countries. These DEA applications have used DMUs of various forms to evaluate the performance of entities, such as hospitals, the wings of U.S. Air Force aircraft, universities, cities, courts, business firms, and others, including the performance of countries, regions, and so on.

Since DEA in its present form was first introduced in 1978, researchers in a number of fields have quickly recognized that it is an excellent and easily used methodology for modeling operational processes for performance evaluations. This has been accompanied by other developments. For example, in Zhu (2003), a number of DEA spreadsheet models that can be used in performance evaluation and benchmarking are developed. DEA's empirical orientation and the absence of a need for the numerous a priori assumptions that accompany other approaches (such as standard forms of statistical regression analysis) have resulted in its use in a number of studies involving efficient frontier estimation in the governmental and nonprofit sector, the regulated sector, and the private sector. Because it requires very few assumptions, DEA has opened up possibilities for use in cases that have been resistant to other approaches because of the complex (often unknown) nature of the relations between the multiple measures.

Figure 1.1 illustrates the basic concept of DEA and how DEA identifies the efficient frontier and establishes benchmarking standards. In Figure 1.1, the *x*-axis represents the standard deviation and *y*-axis represents the return.

Using linear programming technique, DEA identifies a piecewise linear efficient frontier—the solid line shown in Figure 1.1. No other observed DMUs have a better return-risk combination than those DMUs on the identified DEA efficient frontier. For DMU *D* who is termed as (DEA) inefficient, to improve its efficiency, its risk should be reduced to that of *D'* on the efficient frontier, or its return should be increased to that of *D''*. *D'* or *D''* then is identified as the benchmark for DMU *D*.

In DEA, multiple performance measures are called inputs and outputs. In Figure 1.1, the risk is a DEA input and the return is a DEA output. Usually, the inputs represent measures where smaller values are preferred (for

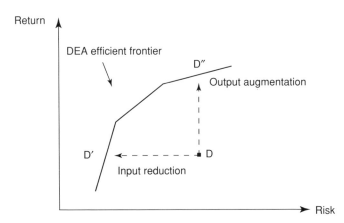

FIGURE 1.1   DEA Efficient Frontier

example, risk measures), and the outputs usually represent measures where larger values are preferred (for example, returns).

Figure 1.1 shows that DEA uses either input reduction or output increase for inefficient DMUs to reach the efficient frontier. The efficient frontier is composed by the DMUs where no input reduction and output increase are necessary. As a result, we have input-oriented DEA models where the inputs are optimized (reduced) while the outputs are kept at their current levels, and output-oriented DEA models where the outputs are optimized (increased) while the inputs are kept at their current levels. We illustrate these two types of DEA models using Figures 1.2 and 1.3.

Figure 1.2 shows five CTAs; each has the same return during one common time period. The two inputs are standard deviation and proportion of monthly negative return. In this example, CTA4 and CTA5 are relatively inefficient. For example, CTA4 has the same standard deviation as CTA2 but has 15% more negative monthly returns. DEA compares all five CTAs based upon the two inputs and the single output and identifies CTA1, CTA2, and CTA3 as the best-practice units. The efficient frontier is represented by the line segments between these three efficient CTAs. DEA identifies T1 on the line segment between CTA1 and CTA2 as the benchmarking standard for the inefficient CTA4.

Figure 1.3 shows five hedge funds HF1 through HF5, assuming they have the same input level (for example, same standard deviation). The two outputs are return and skewness. The output-oriented DEA identifies HF1, HF2, and HF3 as the best-practice units. HF4 and HF5 should increase

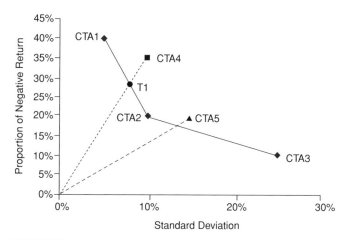

FIGURE 1.2 Input-Oriented DEA

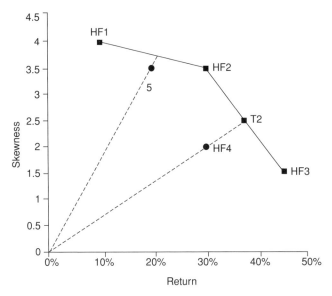

FIGURE 1.3   Output-Oriented DEA

their current output levels with the current amount of input. T2 is the benchmarking standard for HF4.

From this discussion, it can be seen that DEA uses the following definition to identify the efficient frontier (Cooper, Seiford, and Zhu, 2004).

> *Definition 1.1 (Relative Efficiency): A DMU is to be rated as efficient on the basis of available evidence if and only if the performances of other DMUs do not show that some of its inputs or outputs can be improved without worsening some of its other inputs or outputs.*

Cooper, Seiford, and Zhu (2004) point out that this definition avoids the need for recourse to prices or other assumptions of weights that are supposed to reflect the relative importance of the different inputs or outputs. It also avoids the need for explicitly specifying the formal relations that are supposed to exist between inputs and outputs with various types of models, such as linear and nonlinear regression models. This basic kind of efficiency, referred to as "technical efficiency" in economics can be extended, however, to other kinds of efficiency when data such as prices, unit costs, and so on, are available for use in DEA.

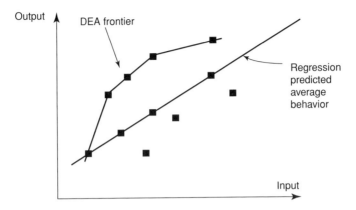

FIGURE 1.4   DEA and Regression

DEA is originally described as a "mathematical programming model applied to observational data [that] provides a new way of obtaining empirical estimates of relations—such as the production functions and/or efficient production possibility surfaces—that are cornerstones of modern economics" (Charnes, Cooper, and Rhodes, 1978). In fact, DEA is a methodology directed to frontiers rather than central tendencies. Instead of trying to fit a regression plane through the center of the data as in statistical regression, for example, one "floats" a piecewise linear surface to rest on top of the observations, as shown in Figure 1.4.

DEA provides basic benchmarking information that includes (1) an efficiency score for each DMU, (2) an efficiency reference set with peer DMUs, (3) a target for inefficient DMU, and (4) information detailing by how much inputs can be decreased or outputs can be increased to improve performance. As a result, we have an efficient frontier consisting of best-practice units and a projection to the frontier that can be used as a "what to do" guide for fund managers. The efficiency reference set is composed by efficient DMUs that are used to construct the target, or benchmarking standard, for inefficient DMUs (for example, the efficiency reference set for CTA5 in Figure 1.2 consists of CTA2 and CTA3). Therefore, DEA provides a fair benchmarking tool.

CHAPTER 2

DEA Models

INTRODUCTION

Regression-based methods can be used in evaluating performance of a set of Decision Making Units (DMUs). However, they are limited to only one dependent variable. For example, $y = \beta_o + \sum_{i=1}^{m} \beta_i x_i + \varepsilon$, where β_i are estimated coefficients that can be used to determine whether an independent variable has a positive effect on the dependent variable or makes an important contribution. The estimated regression line can be served as the benchmark in the performance evaluation, where x_i are inputs and y is the output. However, we are very likely to have multiple outputs y_r $(r = 1, \ldots, s)$. We may have $\sum_{r=1}^{s} u_r y_r = \alpha + \sum_{i=1}^{m} v_i x_i$, where u_r and v_i are unknown weights representing the relative importance or tradeoffs among y_r and x_i.

Suppose we estimate u_r and v_i, then for each DMU_j, we can define

$$h_j = \frac{\alpha + \sum_{i=1}^{m} v_i x_{ij}}{\sum_{r=1}^{s} u_r y_{rj}}$$

as a performance index, where x_{ij}, $(i = 1, 2, \ldots, m)$ are multiple inputs, y_{rj}, $(r = 1, 2, \ldots, s)$ are multiple outputs for DMU_j; $j = 1, 2, \ldots, n$.

In order to estimate u_r and v_i, and further evaluate the performance of j_oth DMU, (denoted as DMU_o), DEA uses the following linear fractional programming problem

$$h_o^* = \min_{\alpha, v_i, u_r} \frac{\alpha + \sum_{i=1}^{m} v_i x_{io}}{\sum_{r=1}^{s} u_r y_{ro}}$$

subject to

$$h_j = \frac{\alpha + \sum_{i=1}^{m} v_i x_{ij}}{\sum_{r=1}^{s} u_r y_{rj}} \geq 1, j = 1, \ldots, n \qquad (2.1)$$

α free in sign and $u_r, v_i \geq 0 \quad \forall \ r, i$

where, x_{io} and y_{ro} are respectively the ith input and rth output for DMU_o under evaluation.

It is clear from the above model that a smaller value of h_o^* is preferred since we prefer larger values of y_{ro} and smaller values of x_{io}. Therefore, this data envelopment analysis (DEA) model tries to find a set of weights v_i and u_r so that the ratio of aggregated x_{io} to aggregated y_{ro} reaches the minimum. Because of the constraints $h_j \geq 1$, the optimal value to (2.1) or the minimum h_o, must be equal to or greater than one. Obviously, a score of one represents the best, that is, if the unity value is achieved for DMU_o ($h_o^* = 1$), then DMU_o is efficient or on the frontier in terms of the given multiple performance measures. Otherwise, if $h_o^* > 1$, then DMU_o is inefficient.

Note that model (2.1) is solved for each unit. Therefore, model (2.1) does not seek the average best performance, but the efficient or best performance achievable by a set of optimized weights.

Note that when $h_o^* = 1$, we have $\sum_{r=1}^{s} u_r^* y_{ro} = \alpha^* + \sum_{i=1}^{m} v_i^* x_{io}$, where (*) represents the optimal values in model (2.1). That is, DEA has estimated the "coefficients." α^* can be regarded as the intercept on the y-axis. It can be seen that while the regression estimates one set of coefficients, DEA model (2.1) estimates one set of coefficients for each DMU, resulting a piecewise linear tradeoff curve associated with efficient DMUs (see Figure 1.1 in Chapter 1).

The next section shows how to use linear programming technique to solve the DEA ratio model (2.1) and provides a number of equivalent basic DEA models.

DEA MODEL CALCULATION

We use $t = \dfrac{1}{\sum\limits_{r=1}^{s} u_r y_{ro}}$, $\omega_i = t v_i$, $\omega_o = t\alpha$, $\mu_r = t u_r$ to convert the model

(2.1) into an equivalent linear programming problem

$$\min_{\omega_o, \omega_i, \mu_r} \; \omega_o + \sum_{i=1}^{m} \omega_i x_{io}$$

subject to

$$\sum_{r=1}^{s} \mu_r y_{rj} - \sum_{i=1}^{m} \omega_i x_{ij} - \omega_o \leq 0 \forall j$$

$$\sum_{r=1}^{s} \mu_r y_{ro} = 1 \qquad\qquad (2.2)$$

$$\mu_r, \omega_i \geq 0 \forall r, i$$

Model (2.2) is called a multiplier DEA model where ω_i and μ_r are input and output multipliers. A number of software packages are available to solve linear programs. For example, the Microsoft® Excel Solver is a spreadsheet optimizer that can be used to solve model (2.2). The current book provides an Excel Add-In for our DEA models.

Model (2.2) can be solved by its dual program

$$\phi_o^* = \max \; \phi_o$$

subject to

$$\sum_{j=1}^{n} \lambda_j x_{ij} \leq x_{io} \qquad\qquad i = 1, 2, ..., m;$$

$$\sum_{j=1}^{n} \lambda_j y_{rj} \geq \phi_o y_{ro} \qquad\qquad r = 1, 2, ..., s; \qquad (2.3)$$

$$\sum_{j=1}^{n} \lambda_j = 1$$

$$\lambda_j \geq 0 \qquad\qquad j = 1, ..., n.$$

Model (2.3) tries to see if the output value can be increased by maximizing the objective function, that is, model (2.3) is an output-oriented

DEA model. In DEA, model (2.3) is called an envelopment model, because it identifies the efficient frontier that envelops all the observations (DMUs). We have (i) if the optimal value to (2.3) $\phi_o^* = 1$, then the DMU_o under evaluation is efficient and $\lambda_o^* = 1$ and $\lambda_j^* = 0$ ($j \neq o$) and (ii) if $\phi_o^* \neq 1$ (i.e., $\phi_o^* > 1$), then DMU_o is inefficient, and $\lambda_o^* = 0$ and some $\lambda_j^* \neq 0$ ($j \neq o$). These non-zero optimal λ_j^* provides the benchmarks for inefficient DMUs.

Consider Figure 2.1 where we have 5 DMUs (A, B, C, D, and E) with one input and one output. Based upon model (2.3), E's current output value can be increased to C's. Therefore, the optimal value to (2.3) for E, ϕ_E^*, is greater than one, indicating E is an inefficient DMU. C however, is an efficient DMU and the optimal value to (2.3) for C, $\phi_C^* = 1$, because C's current output value cannot be increased when compared to the existing DMUs or any convex combinations of the existing DMUs. The same can be said for DMUs A, B, and D.

The constraint $\sum_{j=1}^{n} \lambda_j = 1$ indicates that any convex combinations of the DMUs are either on or enveloped by the efficient frontier. This convexity constraint is related to the returns-to-scale (RTS) concept and estimation in DEA. In DEA, the frontier in Figure 2.1 exhibits variable returns-to-scale (VRS), where AB exhibits increasing RTS (IRS), B exhibits constant RTS (CRS), and BC and CD exhibit decreasing RTS (DRS). Such RTS classifications can be used to classify the hedge funds and CTAs (see discussions in

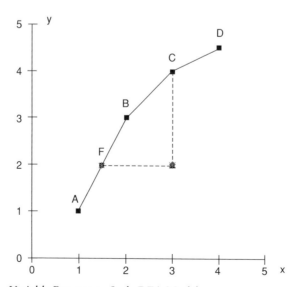

FIGURE 2.1   Variable Returns-to-Scale DEA Model

Chapter 3). Therefore, model (2.3) is called (output-oriented) VRS envelopment model.

We next apply the output-oriented VRS DEA model to the hedge fund example shown in Figure 1.3. Suppose we consider the performance of HF4, we have

$$\max \phi$$

subject to

$$1\lambda_1 + 1\lambda_2 + 1\lambda_3 + 1\lambda_4 + 1\lambda_5 \leq 1 \quad \text{(same input level)}$$
$$10\%\lambda_1 + 30\%\lambda_2 + 45\%\lambda_3 + 30\%\lambda_4 + 20\%\lambda_5 \geq 30\%\phi$$
$$4\lambda_1 + 3.5\lambda_2 + 1.5\lambda_3 + 2\lambda_4 + 3.5\lambda_5 \geq 2\phi$$
$$\lambda_1 + \lambda_2 + \lambda_3 + \lambda_4 + \lambda_5 = 1$$
$$\lambda_1, \lambda_2, \lambda_3, \lambda_4, \lambda_5 \geq 0$$

which yields a set of optimal solutions $\phi^* = 1.25$, $\lambda_2^* = \lambda_3^* = 0.5$, and all other variables zero. This indicates that HF4 is inefficient when compared to benchmarks HF2 and HF3.

If we use the input-oriented VRS DEA model, DMU E in Figure 1.2 will be compared to F, a convex combination of A and B, that is, E should reduce its input to F, or F is the efficient target/benchmarking standard for E. The algebraic formula for the input-oriented VRS DEA model can be expressed as

$$\theta^* = \min \theta$$

subject to

$$\sum_{j=1}^{n} \lambda_j x_{ij} \leq \theta x_{io} \qquad i = 1, 2, \ldots, m;$$

$$\sum_{j=1}^{n} \lambda_j y_{rj} \geq y_{ro} \qquad r = 1, 2, \ldots, s; \qquad (2.4)$$

$$\sum_{j=1}^{n} \lambda_j = 1$$

$$\lambda_j \geq 0 \qquad j = 1, 2, \ldots, n.$$

We have (i) if the optimal value to (2.4) $\theta_o^* = 1$, then DMU_o is efficient and $\lambda_o^* = 1$ and $\lambda_j^* = 0$ ($j \neq o$) and (ii) if $\theta_o^* \neq 1$ (i.e., $\theta_o^* < 1$), then DMU_o is inefficient, and $\lambda_o^* = 0$ and some $\lambda_j^* \neq 0$ ($j \neq o$). These non-zero optimal λ_j^* provide the benchmarks for inefficient DMUs.

Consider the CTA example in Figure 1.2 in Chapter 1. Applying model (2.4) to CTA4 yields

$$\min \theta$$

subject to

$$5\%\lambda_1 + 10\%\lambda_2 + 25\%\lambda_3 + 10\%\lambda_4 + 15\%\lambda_5 \leq 10\%\theta$$
$$40\%\lambda_1 + 20\%\lambda_2 + 10\%\lambda_3 + 35\%\lambda_4 + 20\%\lambda_5 \leq 35\%\theta$$
$$\lambda_1 + \lambda_2 + \lambda_3 + \lambda_4 + \lambda_5 \geq 1 \quad \text{(Same output level)}$$
$$\lambda_1 + \lambda_2 + \lambda_3 + \lambda_4 + \lambda_5 = 1$$
$$\lambda_1, \lambda_2, \lambda_3, \lambda_4, \lambda_5 \geq 0$$

and $\theta^* = 0.8$, $\lambda_1^* = 0.4$, $\lambda_2^* = 0.6$, and all other variables zero. This indicates that CTA4 is inefficient when compared to benchmarks CTA1 and CTA2.

Note that DEA benchmarks are not risk factors but rather efficient funds as defined in input-output measures, where each measure represents risk and return criteria (Wilkens and Zhu, 2003). When an envelopment DEA model is solved, the benchmark (or target) is given by

$$\begin{cases} \displaystyle\sum_{j=1}^{n} \lambda_j^* x_{ij}, & i = 1, \ldots, m \\ \\ \displaystyle\sum_{j=1}^{n} \lambda_j^* y_{rj}, & r = 1, \ldots, s \end{cases} \tag{2.5}$$

where (*) represents optimal values.

The input-oriented VRS DEA model is equivalent to the following DEA (ratio) model

$$\max_{\alpha, v_i, u_r} \frac{\displaystyle\sum_{r=1}^{s} u_r y_{ro} + \alpha}{\displaystyle\sum_{i=1}^{m} v_i x_{io}}$$

subject to

$$\frac{\displaystyle\sum_{r=1}^{s} u_r y_{rj} + \alpha}{\displaystyle\sum_{i=1}^{m} v_i x_{ij}} \leq 1, j = 1, \ldots, n$$

α free in sign and $u_r, v_i \geq 0 \quad \forall r, i$

and its dual linear program is

$$\max \sum_{r=1}^{s} \mu_r y_{ro} + \mu$$

subject to

$$\sum_{r=1}^{s} \mu_r y_{rj} - \sum_{i=1}^{m} v_i x_{ij} + \mu \leq 0$$

$$\sum_{i=1}^{m} v_i x_{io} = 1$$

$$\mu \text{ free in sign, } \mu_r, v_i \geq 0$$

MARKOWITZ MODEL AND SHARPE RATIO

The first portfolio selection model to deal explicitly with return and risk is developed by Markowitz (1952). An investor chooses among all possible portfolios in terms of portfolio risk and return. The basic selection rule is to choose the efficient portfolios that offer the least risk for a given return. Markowitz (1959) defines a set of legitimate portfolios that can be obtained from a set of N securities, $X_j \geq 0$ $(j = 1, \ldots, N)$, where $\sum_{j=1}^{N} X_j = 1$. Different combinations of X_j yield various portfolio returns (E_k) and variances (or standard deviations, σ_k). When a set of portfolios are given, we may (i) use "critical line algorithm" of Markowitz (1959) or (ii) plot the portfolios to identify the efficient portfolio frontier. In fact, either the input-oriented or output-oriented VRS DEA model can be used to identify the efficient portfolio frontier.

We have

$$\max \phi$$

subject to

$$\sum_k \lambda_k E_k \geq \phi E_o$$

$$\sum_k {}_k \sigma_k \leq \sigma_o$$

$$\sum_k {}_k = 1$$

where our objective is to find the maximum return given the standard deviation, or

$$\min \phi$$

subject to

$$\sum_{k} \lambda_k E_k \geq E_o$$

$$\sum_{k} \lambda_k \sigma_k \leq \theta \sigma_o$$

$$\sum_{k} \lambda_k = 1$$

where our objective is to find the minimum standard deviation given the expected return.

The above are two single input-single output DEA models and the DEA efficient portfolio frontier is piecewise linear as shown in Markowitz (1952).

The Markowitz portfolio selection model identifies all efficient portfolios. But we still have not given the investor directions as how to choose his or her specific efficient portfolio (or a benchmark) to invest. Usually, this choice depends on the investor's appetite for risk. For example, a risk-taker may prefer a portfolio with greater standard deviation and commensurately higher returns. If one assumes that a portfolio manager does not want to (i) increase its current risk and (ii) decrease its current return, then DEA has the advantage in providing the benchmark via $\left(\sum_{k} \lambda_k^* E_k, \sum_{k} \lambda_k^* \sigma_k \right)$ in the optimal solutions to DEA model. When the preference information on return and risk is available, we can use other DEA models for an inefficient portfolio to find a benchmark.

The Markowitz model identifies all the efficient portfolios. Sharpe ratio, by contrast, identifies one efficient portfolio via a ratio of differential return to risk:

$$S = \frac{\overline{E}}{\sigma} = \frac{E - E_B}{\sigma}$$

where E_B is the return on a benchmark portfolio or security.

Note that in Figure 2.1, A, B, C, and D represent the Markowitz frontier. Only B is efficient under the Sharpe ratio model. The Sharpe ratio

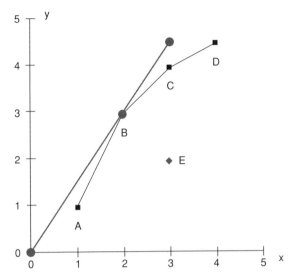

FIGURE 2.2   Constant DEA Model

frontier is ray *OB* as shown in Figure 2.2. In the next section, we introduce DEA models that identify such types of efficient frontier.

CONSTANT RETURNS-TO-SCALE DEA MODEL

In DEA, a frontier like ray *OB* is said to be exhibiting constant returns-to-scale (CRS) and the associated DEA model is called CRS model. The CRS DEA model is obtained if we drop the convexity $\sum_{j=1}^{n} \lambda_j = 1$ from the VRS DEA model. The input-oriented CRS (envelopment) model is

$$\min \theta$$

subject to

$$\sum_{j=1}^{n} \lambda_j x_{ij} \leq \theta x_{io} \qquad i = 1, 2, \ldots, m;$$

$$\sum_{j=1}^{n} \lambda_j y_{rj} \geq y_{ro} \qquad r = 1, 2, \ldots, s; \qquad (2.6)$$

$$\lambda_j \geq 0 \qquad j = 1, 2, \ldots, n.$$

The output-oriented CRS (envelopment) DEA model is

$$\max \theta$$

subject to

$$\sum_{j=1}^{n} \lambda_j x_{ij} \leq x_{io} \qquad i = 1, 2, \ldots, n$$

$$\sum_{j=1}^{n} \lambda_j y_{rj} \geq \phi y_{ro} \qquad r = 1, 2, \ldots, s; \qquad (2.7)$$

$$\lambda_j \geq 0 \qquad j = 1, 2, \ldots, n.$$

In the context of the CRS DEA model, the Sharpe ratio is equivalent to

$$\max \tilde{\phi}$$

subject to

$$\sum_k \lambda_k \overline{E}_k \geq \tilde{\phi} \overline{E}_o \quad \text{or}$$

$$\sum_k \lambda_k \sigma_k \leq \sigma_o$$

or

$$\min \tilde{\theta}$$

subject to

$$\sum_k \lambda_k \overline{E}_k \geq \overline{E}_o$$

$$\sum_k \lambda_k \sigma_k \leq \tilde{\theta} \sigma_o$$

The input-oriented CRS DEA model is equivalent to the following ratio DEA model

$$\max_{v_i, u_r} \frac{\sum_{r=1}^{s} u_r y_{ro}}{\sum_{i=1}^{m} v_i x_{io}}$$

subject to

$$\frac{\sum_{r=1}^{s} u_r y_{rj}}{\sum_{i=1}^{m} v_i x_{ij}} \leq 1, j = 1, \ldots, n$$

$$u_r, v_i \geq 0 \quad \forall \, r, i$$

It is a ratio of weighted outputs to inputs. It is clear that this DEA extends the single output to input ratio to a case where multiple inputs and outputs are present without the need for specifying the weights. DEA determines a set of weights for each DMU under evaluation to best reflect the DMU's performance through linear programming optimization.

The output-oriented CRS DEA model is equivalent to

$$\min_{v_i, u_r} \frac{\sum_{i=1}^{m} v_i x_{io}}{\sum_{r=1}^{s} u_r y_{ro}}$$

subject to

$$\frac{\sum_{i=1}^{m} v_i x_{ij}}{\sum_{r=1}^{s} u_r y_{rj}} \geq 1, j = 1, \ldots, n$$

$$u_r, v_i \geq 0 \quad \forall r, i$$

It is obvious that the efficiency scores of the input- and output-oriented CRS DEA models are reciprocal. However, the two models will yield different benchmarks for an inefficient DMU under evaluation, because of the different orientations with respect to input decrease and output increase.

NEGATIVE DATA

One requirement in the above DEA models is that values of x_{ij} and y_{rj} must not be negative. However, it is very likely that, for example, returns on some hedge funds and CTAs are negative, that is, we have cases where some inputs and outputs have negative values. This can be easily solved by the *translation invariance property* of the VRS models.

Suppose x_{ij} and y_{rj} are displaced by $\beta \geq 0$ and $\pi_r \geq 0$, respectively. Now we have a set of new values on x_{ij} and y_{rj}

$$\begin{cases} \hat{x}_{ij} = x_{ij} + \beta_i \\ \hat{y}_{rj} = y_{rj} + \pi_r \end{cases}$$

Note that the efficient frontier is determined by units with $\phi_o^* = 1$ or $\theta_o^* = 1$. Note also that $\sum_{j=1}^{n} \lambda_j = 1$ in the VRS envelopment models. Therefore, the efficient frontier remains the same if x_{ij} and y_{rj} are replaced by $\hat{x}_{ij}$ and $\hat{y}_{rj}$, respectively. As a result, the VRS models can deal with negative data.

However, the input-oriented VRS model's optimal solutions are invariant to output changes, and the output-oriented VRS model's optimal solutions are invariant to input changes. Thus, if we have negative input data, the output-oriented VRS model is a better choice; if we have negative output data, the input-oriented VRS model is a better choice. If we have both negative input and output data, we can use either of the VRS models. However, we must note that when the negative data are transformed into positive ones, the efficient frontier under the VRS models remains unchanged.

Consider the example use in Wilkens and Zhu (2001) where we have two inputs x_1 = Standard Deviation and x_2 = PropNeg (proportion of negative monthly returns during the year), and three outputs y_1 = Return (average monthly return), y_2 = Skewness, and y_3 = Min (minimum return) (see Table 2.1).

Note that some values on return, skewness, and Min are negative. Therefore the average monthly return, skewness, and minimum return are displaced by 3.7%, 2, and 26%, respectively, so that all the output values are positive across all the CTAs. The translation values can be chosen randomly as long as the negative values become positive.

Because only the outputs have negative data and are transformed into positive values, we use the input-oriented VRS model. When CTA1 is under evaluation, we have $\theta_o^* = 0.75$, indicating this CTA is inefficient, and $\lambda_3^* = 0.51$ and $\lambda_4^* = 0.49$, indicating CTA3 and CTA4 are the benchmarks.

DEAFrontier EXCEL ADD-IN

This book provides a DEA software called *DEAFrontier*. *DEAFrontier* is an Add-In for Microsoft Excel and uses the Excel Solver. This software requires Excel 97 or later versions.

DEAFrontier does not set any limit on the number of units, inputs, or outputs. It is only limited by the Excel Solver one uses. Please check www.solver.com for problem sizes that various versions of Excel Solver can handle (see Table 2.2).

To install the software the CD-ROM using Windows, follow these steps:

1. Insert the CD-ROM into your computer's CD-ROM drive. (If the auto run does not execute, follow steps 2 through 4.)
2. Launch Windows Explore.
3. Click Browse to browse the CD and find the file "Setup.exe."
4. Run "Setup.exe."

TABLE 2.1 Negative Data Example

| CTA | | Original Data | | | | Transformed Data $\hat{y}_r = y_{rij} + \pi_r$ | | |
	$x_1 =$ Standard Deviation	$x_2 =$ Proportion Negative	$y_1 =$ Ave. Monthly Return	$y_2 =$ Skewness	$y_3 =$ Minimum Return	$\hat{y}_1$; $\pi_1 = 3.7\%$	$\hat{y}_2$; $\pi_2 = 2$	$\hat{y}_3$; $\pi_3 = 26\%$
1	6.80%	58.30%	0.10%	1.13	-8.10%	3.80%	3.13	17.90%
2	4.00%	41.70%	0.70%	0.61	-7.90%	4.40%	2.61	18.10%
3	3.40%	37.50%	0.90%	0.58	-4.00%	4.60%	2.58	22.00%
4	5.00%	50.00%	0.60%	1.7	-5.60%	4.30%	3.7	20.40%
5	4.70%	37.50%	1.10%	0.28	-8.20%	4.80%	2.28	17.80%
6	3.80%	50.00%	-0.10%	0.08	-6.30%	3.60%	2.08	19.70%
7	11.20%	45.80%	3.20%	0.39	-17.10%	6.90%	2.39	8.90%
8	12.80%	58.30%	-1.00%	0.46	-25.70%	2.70%	2.46	0.30%
9	8.40%	52.20%	-1.20%	-0.26	-17.10%	2.50%	1.74	8.90%
9	5.00%	54.50%	0.40%	1.1	-6.70%	4.10%	3.1	19.30%
10	8.60%	25.00%	-3.60%	-1.98	-16.50%	0.10%	0.02	9.50%

TABLE 2.2 Microsoft Excel Solver Problem Size

Problem Size:	Standard Problem Size:	Premium Solver	Premium Solver Platform
Variables × Constraints	200 × 200	1000 × 8000	2000 × 8000

Source: www.solver.com

To run *DEAFrontier*, the Excel Solver must first be installed, and the Solver parameter dialog box must be displayed at least once in the Excel session. Otherwise, an error may occur when you run the software, as shown in Figure 2.3. Please also make sure that the Excel Solver works properly. One can use the file "solvertest.xls" to test whether the Excel Solver works. This test file is also available at www.deafrontier.com/solvertest.xls.

You may follow these steps.

First, in Excel, invoke the Solver by using the Tools/Solver menu item as shown in Figure 2.4. This will load the Solver parameter dialog box as shown in Figure 2.5. Then close the Solver parameter dialog box by clicking the Close button. Now you have successfully loaded the Excel Solver.

If Solver does not exist in the Tools menu, you need to select Tools/Add-Ins, and check the Solver box, as shown in Figure 2.6. (If Solver does not show in the Add-Ins, you need to install the Solver first.)

Next, load *DEAFrontier* software, and a "*DEAFrontier*" menu is added at the end of the Excel menu (see Figure 2.7).

FIGURE 2.3 Error Message

FIGURE 2.4   Display Solver Parameters Dialog Box

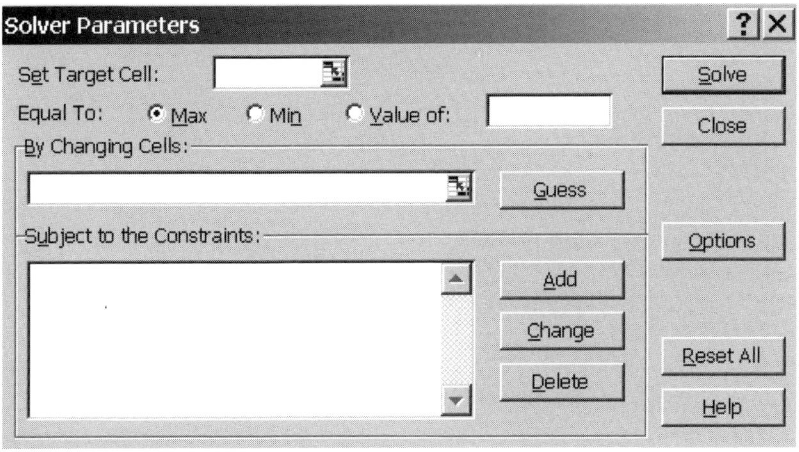

FIGURE 2.5   Solver Parameters Dialog Box

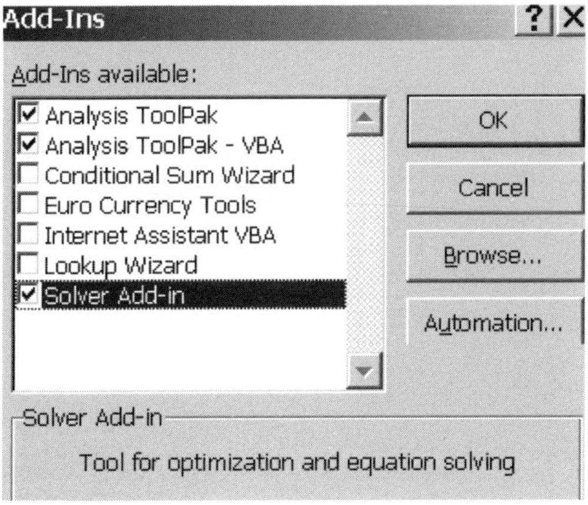

FIGURE 2.6   Solver Add-In

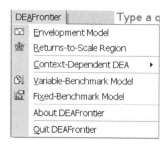

FIGURE 2.7   *DEAFrontier* Menu

The data sheet containing the data for funds (or DMUs) under evaluations must be named as "Data." The data sheet should have the format as shown in Figure 2.8.

Leave one blank column between the input and output data. No blank columns and rows are allowed within the input and output data. See Figure 2.9 for an example.

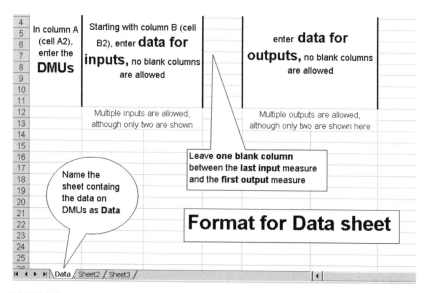

FIGURE 2.8   Data Sheet Format

	A	B	C	D	E	F	G
1	CTA	Standard Deviation	Proportion Negative		Monthly Return	Skewness	Minimum Return
2	CTA1	6.80%	58.30%		3.80%	3.13	17.90%
3	CTA2	4.00%	41.70%		4.40%	2.61	18.10%
4	CTA3	3.40%	37.50%		4.60%	2.58	22.00%
5	CTA4	5.00%	50.00%		4.30%	3.7	20.40%
6	CTA5	4.70%	37.50%		4.80%	2.28	17.80%
7	CTA6	3.80%	50.00%		3.60%	2.08	19.70%
8	CTA7	11.20%	45.80%		6.90%	2.39	8.90%
9	CTA8	12.80%	58.30%		2.70%	2.46	0.30%
10	CTA9	8.40%	52.20%		2.50%	1.74	8.90%
11	CTA10	5.00%	54.50%		4.10%	3.1	19.30%
12	CTA11	8.60%	25.00%		0.10%	0.02	9.50%
13							
14							

FIGURE 2.9   Sample Data Sheet

Negative or non-numerical data are deemed as invalid data. The software checks that the data are in valid form before the calculation. If the data sheet contains negative or non-numerical data, the software quits and locates the invalid data (see Figure 2.10). If negative data are present, one must translate the negative data first as discussed in the section called "Negative Data."

	A	B	C	D	E	F
1	CTA	Standard Deviation	Proportion Negative		Monthly Return	Skewness	Mini
2	1	6.80%	58.30%		3.80%	3.13
3	2	-4.00%	41.70%		4.40%	2.61
4	3	3.40%	37.50%		4.60%	2.58
5	4	5.00%	50.00%		4.30%	3.7
6	5	4.70%	37.50%				
7	6	3.80%	50.00%				
8	7	11.20%	45.80%				
9	8	12.80%	58.30%				
10	9	8.40%	52.20%				
11	9	5.00%	54.50%				
12	10	8.60%	25.00%				
13							

DEAFrontier Error ✕

Invalid input value is detected at 1th input of DMU 2
Please edit the Data Sheet.

OK

FIGURE 2.10   Invalid Data

SOLVING DEA MODEL

To run the envelopment models, select the "Envelopment Model" menu item. You will be prompted with a form for selecting the models, as shown in Figure 2.11.

Model Orientation refers to whether a DEA model is input-oriented, or output-oriented, and Frontier Type refers to the returns-to-scale type of the DEA efficient frontier. For example, if you select "Input-Oriented" and "VRS," then model (2.4) will be used. If you select "Output-Oriented" and "CRS," then model (2.7) will be used.

Suppose we use the default selection of "Input-Oriented" and "CRS," that is, model (2.6). The software reports the results in two sheets. The "Efficiency" sheet reports the input and output names. Column A reports the DMU number and Column B reports the fund names. Column C reports the efficiency scores (it also indicates the type of DEA models used). Column D reports the optimal $\Sigma\lambda_j^*$ which is used to identify the returns-to-scale classifications reported in column E (see the next chapter for discussions on returns-to-scale). Sheet "Efficiency" also reports the benchmark DMUs along with the optimal λ_j^*. Figure 2.12 presents the results of the data shown in Figure 2.7. Consider CTA1. Its DEA efficiency score is 0.73 when compared to CTA3 and CTA4. The number to the left of the two bench-

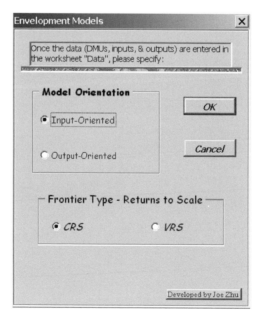

FIGURE 2.11   Envelopment Model

	A	B	C	D	E	F	G	H	I	J	K
1	Inputs		Outputs								
2	Standard Deviation		Monthly Return								
3	Proportion Negative		Skewness								
4			Minimum Return								
5											
6			Input-Oriented								
7			CRS								
8	DMU No.	DMU Name	Efficiency	$\Sigma\lambda$	RTS	Benchmarks					
9	1	CTA1	0.73010	0.877	Increasing		0.101	CTA3		0.775	CTA4
10	2	CTA2	0.89974	0.964	Increasing		0.853	CTA3		0.110	CTA4
11	3	CTA3	1.00000	1.000	Constant		1.000	CTA3			
12	4	CTA4	1.00000	1.000	Constant		1.000	CTA4			
13	5	CTA5	0.99246	0.952	Increasing		0.769	CTA3		0.183	CTA7
14	6	CTA6	0.80120	0.895	Increasing		0.895	CTA3			
15	7	CTA7	1.00000	1.000	Constant		1.000	CTA7			
16	8	CTA8	0.57021	0.665	Increasing		0.665	CTA4			
17	9	CTA9	0.46551	0.561	Increasing		0.298	CTA3		0.262	CTA4
18	10	CTA10	0.81961	1.157	Decreasing		1.054	CTA3		0.103	CTA4
19	11	CTA11	0.64773	0.432	Increasing		0.432	CTA3			

FIGURE 2.12 Efficiency Sheet

mark CTAs, namely, 0.101 and 0.775, represent optimal λ_j^*. This "Efficiency" sheet also reports **1.** the returns-to-scale (RTS) classification and the $\sum \lambda_j^*$ (see Chapter 3 for a detailed discussion), **2.** the inputs and outputs used, and **3.** the DEA model selected.

Sheet "Target" reports the values represented in (2.5). For example, as shown in Figure 2.13, the targets for CTA1's inputs and outputs are 4.22%, 42.57%, 3.8%, 3.13%, and 18.05%, respectively. This CTA will be efficient. There values can also be used as benchmarks.

	A	B	C	D	F	G	H
1	Inputs		Outputs				
2	Standard Deviation		Monthly Return				
3	Proportion Negative		Skewness				
4			Minimum Return				
5							
6	Input-Oriented						
7	CRS Model Target						
8			*Efficient Input Target*		*Efficient Output Target*		
9	DMU No.	DMU Name	*Standard Deviation*	*Proportion Negative*	*Monthly Return*	Skewness	Minimum Return
10	1	CTA1	0.04221	0.42565	0.03800	3.13000	0.18046
11	2	CTA2	0.03453	0.37519	0.04400	2.61000	0.21025
12	3	CTA3	0.03400	0.37500	0.04600	2.58000	0.22000
13	4	CTA4	0.05000	0.50000	0.04300	3.70000	0.20400
14	5	CTA5	0.04665	0.37217	0.04800	2.42123	0.18544
15	6	CTA6	0.03045	0.33580	0.04119	2.31027	0.19700
16	7	CTA7	0.11200	0.45800	0.06900	2.39000	0.08900
17	8	CTA8	0.03324	0.33243	0.02859	2.46000	0.13563
18	9	CTA9	0.02326	0.24300	0.02500	1.74000	0.11913
19	10	CTA10	0.04098	0.44669	0.05290	3.10000	0.25285
20	11	CTA11	0.01468	0.16193	0.01986	1.11409	0.09500

FIGURE 2.13 Target Sheet

Classification Methods

INTRODUCTION

As noted in Wilkens and Zhu (2003), hedge funds, managed futures, and other actively managed funds have neither a universally accepted performance evaluation methodology nor a consistent classification system. Hedge funds and other dynamic strategies are difficult to classify quantitatively for a variety of reasons, including changing fund risk and skewed return distributions. This chapter introduces DEA-based quantitative classification methodology for investment funds that is based on multiple performance measures. It may be suitable for alternative investments for which strategy classifications are now largely qualitative and subjective rather than quantitative. Self-reported (qualitative) hedge fund styles have been shown to be useful in explaining and predicting hedge fund returns, but problems using them include mistaken and potentially deliberate misclassification. For example, Brown and Goetzmann (1997) find evidence of mutual funds switching their classification only to look better relative to their peers (Wilkens and Zhu, 2003).

DEA classifies funds based upon multiple criteria. This is distinctly different from multifactor analysis. Recall that DEA benchmarks are not risk factors but rather efficient funds as defined in input-output measures, where each measure represents risk and return criteria. DEA has the advantage of simultaneously affording a classification scheme and performance evaluation technique. The DEA methodology is a promising approach to addressing quantitative hedge fund classification issues.

RETURNS-TO-SCALE CLASSIFICATION

Because the returns-to-scale (RTS) is related to the VRS envelopment model's frontier, we first present the input- and output-oriented VRS envelopment models discussed in Chapter 2.

$$\theta^{VRS*} = \min \; \theta^{VRS}$$

subject to

$$\sum_{j=1}^{n} \lambda_j x_{ij} \leq \theta^{VRS} x_{io} \qquad i = 1, 2, \ldots, m;$$

$$\sum_{j=1}^{n} \lambda_j y_{rj} \geq y_{ro} \qquad r = 1, 2, \ldots, s; \tag{3.1}$$

$$\sum_{j=1}^{n} \lambda_j = 1$$

$$\lambda_j \geq 0 \qquad j = 1, 2, \ldots, n.$$

$$\phi^{VRS*} = \min \; \phi^{VRS}$$

subject to

$$\sum_{j=1}^{n} \lambda_j x_{ij} \leq x_{io} \qquad i = 1, 2, \ldots, m;$$

$$\sum_{j=1}^{n} \lambda_j y_{rj} \geq \phi^{CRS} y_{ro} \qquad r = 1, 2, \ldots, s; \tag{3.2}$$

$$\sum_{j=1}^{n} \lambda_j = 1$$

$$\lambda_j \geq 0 \qquad j = 1, \ldots, n.$$

The classification technique is based upon the returns-to-scale (RTS) estimation in DEA. RTS have typically been defined only for single output situations. For example, RTS are considered to be increasing if a proportional increase in all the inputs results in a more than proportional increase in the single output. Let α represent the proportional input increase and β represent the resulted proportional increase on the single output. Increasing returns-to-scale prevail if $\beta > \alpha$ and decreasing returns-to-scale prevail if $\beta < \alpha$. (see, for example, Banker, Cooper, Seiford, Thrall, and Zhu, 2004). DEA extends the RTS concept from the single output case to a multiple outputs case.

RTS Region

Recall that in Chapter 2, model (3.1) or (3.2) exhibit variable returns-to-scale (VRS). In Figure 3.1, AB exhibits increasing RTS (IRS), *BC* exhibits constant RTS (CRS), and *CD* exhibits decreasing RTS (DRS).

On the line segment *CD*, decreasing (DRS) prevail to the right of C. By applying model (3.1) to point *H*, we have a frontier point *H′* on the line segment *AB*, and thus *H* exhibits IRS. However a different RTS classification may be obtained if we use the output-oriented model (3.2). The point *H* is moved onto the line segment *CD* by the output-oriented model (3.2), and thus DRS prevail on the point *H″*. This enable us to classify a set of DMUs into six RTS regions as indicated in Figure 3.2.

They are region "I"—IRS, region "II"—CRS, and region "III"—DRS. In fact, we have six RTS regions as shown in Figure 3.2. Two RTS classifications will be assigned into the remaining regions IV, V, and VI. Region "IV" is of IRS (input-oriented) and of CRS (output-oriented). Region "V" is of CRS (input-oriented) and of DRS (output-oriented). Region "VI" is of IRS (input-oriented) and of DRS (output-oriented).

We should point out that RTS regions here are only used as a tool for classifying the funds. The real meaning of RTS may not be applied to the performance of the funds.

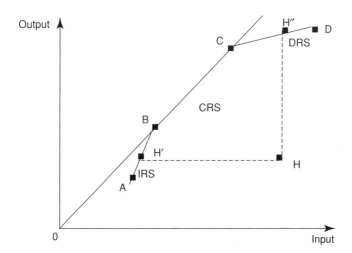

FIGURE 3.1 RTS Frontier

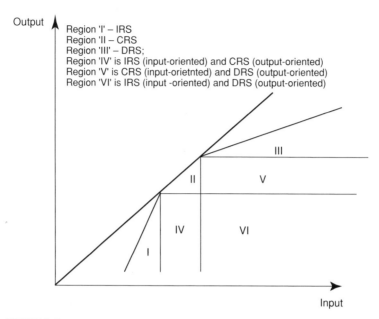

Region 'I' – IRS
Region 'II' – CRS
Region 'III' – DRS;
Region 'IV' is IRS (input-oriented) and CRS (output-oriented)
Region 'V' is CRS (input-orietnted) and DRS (output-oriented)
Region 'VI' is IRS (input -oriented) and DRS (output-oriented)

FIGURE 3.2   RTS Regions

RTS Estimation

We next present the technique for the RTS estimation. For detailed discussion, please see Seiford and Zhu (1999a), Zhu (2003), Banker, Cooper, Seiford, Thrall, and Zhu (2004). Consider the input-oriented CRS envelopment model discussed in Chapter 2 where the constraint of $\sum \lambda_j = 1$ is removed from model (3.1)

$$\theta^{VRS*} = \min \theta^{VRS}$$

subject to

$$\sum_{j=1}^{n} x_{ij}\lambda_j \leq \theta^{VRS} x_{io} \qquad i = 1, 2, \ldots, m;$$

$$\sum_{j=1}^{n} y_{rj}\lambda_j \geq y_{ro} \qquad r = 1, 2, \ldots, s; \tag{3.3}$$

$$\lambda_j \geq 0 \qquad j = 1, 2, \ldots, n.$$

Now, optimal λ_j^* obtained from model (3.3) can be used to estimate the RTS nature of a particular DMU_o as follows (Banker and Thrall, 1992).

1. If $\sum_{j}^{n} \lambda_{j}^{*} = 1$ in *any* alternate optima, then CRS prevail on DMU_{o}.

2. If $\sum_{j}^{n} \lambda_{j}^{*} < 1$ for *all* alternate optima, then IRS prevail on DMU_{o}.

3. If $\sum_{j}^{n} \lambda_{j}^{*} > 1$ for *all* alternate optima, then DRS prevail on DMU_{o}.

It has been recognized that multiple optimal λ_{j}^{*} may be present in model (3.3). In real world applications, the examination of alternative optima is a laborious task, and one may attempt to use a single set of resulting optimal solutions in the application of the RTS methods. However, this may yield erroneous results (Zhu and Shen, 1995). Seiford and Zhu (1999a) show the following results.

Theorem 3.1

1. If DMU_{o} exhibits IRS, then $\sum_{j}^{n} \lambda_{j}^{*} < 1$ for *all* alternate optima.

2. If DMU_{o} exhibits DRS, then $\sum_{j}^{n} \lambda_{j}^{*} > 1$ for *all* alternate optima.

The significance of Theorem 3.1 lies in the fact that the possible alternate optimal λ_{j}^{*} obtained from the CRS envelopment model only affect the estimation of RTS for those DMUs that truly exhibit CRS, and have nothing to do with the RTS estimation on those DMUs that truly exhibit IRS or or DRS. That is, if a DMU exhibits IRS (or DRS), then $\sum_{j}^{n} \lambda_{j}^{*}$ must be less (or greater) than one, even if there exist alternate optima of λ_{j}.

Further, we can have a very simple approach for eliminating the need for examining all alternate optima.

Theorem 3.2

1. θ^{CRS*} (in model (3.3)) is equal to θ^{VRS*} (in model (3.1)) *if and only if* CRS prevail on DMU_{o}. Otherwise,

2. $\sum_{j}^{n} \lambda_{j}^{*} < 1$ *if and only if* IRS prevail on DMU_{o}.

3. $\sum_{j}^{n} \lambda_{j}^{*} > 1$ *if and only if* DRS prevail on DMU_{o}.

Thus, in empirical applications, we can explore RTS in two steps. First, select all the DMUs that have $\theta^{CRS*} = \theta^{VRS*}$ regardless of the value of $\sum_{j}^{n} \lambda_{j}^{*}$. These DMUs are in the CRS region. Next, use the value of $\sum_{j}^{n} \lambda_{j}^{*}$ (in any CRS envelopment model (3.3) outcome) to determine the RTS for the remaining DMUs. We observe that in this process we can safely ignore possible multiple optimal solutions of λ_{j}.

Note that the above discussion is based upon input-oriented DEA models. Similar discussion holds for output-oriented DEA models (see Zhu, 2003). We rewrite the output-oriented CRS envelopment model as follows

$$\phi^{CRS*} = \max \phi^{CRS}$$

subject to

$$\sum_{j=1}^{n} \lambda_j x_{ij} \leq x_{io} \qquad i = 1, 2, \ldots, m;$$

$$\sum_{j=1}^{n} \lambda_j y_{rj} \geq \phi^{CRS} y_{ro} \qquad r = 1, 2, \ldots, s; \qquad (3.4)$$

$$\lambda_j \geq 0 \qquad j = 1, \ldots, n.$$

We have

Theorem 3.3

1. ϕ^{CRS*} (in model (3.4)) is equal to ϕ^{VRS*} (in model (3.2)) *if and only if* CRS prevail on DMU_o. Otherwise,
2. $\sum_{j}^{n} \lambda_j^* < 1$ *if and only if* IRS prevail on DMU_o, where λ_j^* are optimal solutions from the output-oriented CRS envelopment model (3.4);
3. $\sum_{j}^{n} \lambda_j^* > 1$ *if and only if* DRS prevail on DMU_o where λ_j^* are optimal solutions from the output-oriented CRS envelopment model (3.4).

Returns-to-Scale Region Calculation

Based upon Theorems 3.2 and 3.3, the *DEAFrontier* software calculates the returns-to-scale (RTS) regions. To obtain the region, one selects the "Returns-to-Scale Region" menu item, as shown in Figure 3.3. The results

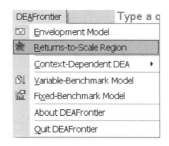

FIGURE 3.3   RTS Region Calculation

			Input-oriented VRS Efficiency	Input-oriented CRS Efficiency	Σλ	Input-oriented RTS	Output-oriented VRS Efficiency	Output-oriented CRS Efficiency	Σλ	Output-oriented RTS
Inputs	Outputs									
Standard Deviation	Monthly Return									
Proportion Negative	Skewness									
	Minimum Return									
DMU No.	DMU Name	RTS Region								
1 CTA1		Region VI	0.74851	0.73010	0.87665	Increasing	1.14404	1.36968	1.20073	Decreasing
2 CTA2		Region VI	0.90731	0.89974	0.96372	Increasing	1.05657	1.11144	1.07111	Decreasing
3 CTA3		Region II	1.00000	1.00000	1.00000	Constant	1.00000	1.00000	1.00000	Constant
4 CTA4		Region II	1.00000	1.00000	1.00000	Constant	1.00000	1.00000	1.00000	Constant
5 CTA5		Region I	1.00000	0.99246	0.95194	Increasing	1.00000	1.00760	0.95917	Increasing
6 CTA6		Region VI	0.89474	0.80120	0.89545	Increasing	1.11675	1.24813	1.11765	Decreasing
7 CTA7		Region II	1.00000	1.00000	1.00000	Constant	1.00000	1.00000	1.00000	Constant
8 CTA8		Region VI	0.63317	0.57021	0.66486	Increasing	1.50407	1.75374	1.16600	Decreasing
9 CTA9		Region VI	0.63982	0.46551	0.56058	Increasing	1.95676	2.14818	1.20423	Decreasing
10 CTA10		Region III	0.82857	0.81961	1.15682	Decreasing	1.07733	1.22009	1.41143	Decreasing
11 CTA11		Region I	1.00000	0.64773	0.43182	Increasing	1.00000	1.54386	0.66667	Increasing

FIGURE 3.4 RTS Regional Result

are reported in sheet "RTS Region." Figure 3.4 shows the RTS region for the CTA data presented in Table 2.1 or Figure 2.7. The "RTS Region" sheet reports the results for Theorems 3.2 and 3.3. For example, consider CTA1. Because the input-oriented CRS and VRS efficiency scores are not equal, the RTS is increasing based upon the fact that $\sum_{j}^{n} \lambda_{j}^{*} = 0.87665 < 1$. However, the output-oriented DEA models indicate that CTA1 is moved onto a DRS frontier. As a result, CTA1 is in Region "VI."

CONTEXT-DEPENDENT DEA

Adding or deleting an inefficient DMU or a set of inefficient DMUs does not alter the efficiencies of the existing DMUs and the efficient frontier. The inefficiency scores change only if the efficient frontier is altered, that is, the performance of DMUs or funds depends only on the identified efficient frontier. Context-dependent DEA is developed by Zhu (2003) and extended by Seiford and Zhu (2003) so that a set of DMUs can be grouped into different subsets with respect to various performance levels. The context-dependent DEA enables the user to compare and benchmark performance in between different DMU groups. This DEA methodology enables decision makers to identify the most attractive unit and the competitive funds in the market. In this section, we present the method developed in Zhu (2003).

Obtain Performance Levels

Context-dependent DEA involves identifying DEA efficient frontiers at different performance levels. These efficient frontiers are then used as evaluation context. To obtain these frontiers, a DEA model is applied to a set of

DMUs when each identified efficient frontier is removed until there is no DMU left. For example, if we apply the CRS envelopment model to the set of CTAs shown in Table 2.1, we have three efficient CTA3, CTA4, and CTA7 as the first-level efficient frontier—the original efficient frontier. Next, we remove the three efficient CTAs and apply the CRS model to the remaining eight CTAs. We have three efficient CTA2, CTA5, and CTA6 as the second-level efficient frontier. This process is continued until no CTA is left in the set. Such a process is carried out by the following algorithm (Zhu, 2003).

Define $\mathbf{J}^1 = \{DMU_j, j = 1, \ldots, n\}$ (the set of all n DMUs) and interactively define $\mathbf{J}^{l+1} = \mathbf{J}^l - \mathbf{E}^l$ where $\mathbf{E}^l = \{DMU_k \in \mathbf{J}^l \mid \theta^*(l, k) = 1\}$, and $\theta^*(l, k)$ is the optimal value to the following input-oriented CRS envelopment model when DMU_k is under evaluation:

$$\theta^*(l, k) = \min_{\lambda_j, \theta(l, k)} \theta(l, k)$$

subject to

$$\sum_{j \in F(\mathbf{J}^l)} \lambda_j x_{ij} \leq \theta(l, k) x_{ik}$$
$$\sum_{j \in F(\mathbf{J}^l)} \lambda_j y_{rj} \geq y_{rk} \qquad (3.5)$$
$$\lambda_j \geq 0 \quad j \in F(\mathbf{J}^l).$$

where $j \in F(\mathbf{J}^l)$ means $DMU_j \in \mathbf{J}^l$, that is, represents the correspondence from a DMU set to the corresponding subscript index set.

When $l = 1$, model (3.5) becomes the original input-oriented CRS envelopment model, and $\mathbf{E}^1$ consists of all the frontier DMUs. These DMUs in set $\mathbf{E}^1$ define the first-level efficient frontier. When $l = 2$, model (3.5) gives the second-level efficient frontier after the exclusion of the first-level efficient frontier DMUs. And so on. In this manner, we identify several levels of efficient E frontiers. We call $\mathbf{E}^l$ the lth-level efficient frontier.

Step 1: Set $l = 1$. Evaluate the entire set of DMUs, $\mathbf{J}^1$, by model (3.5) to obtain the first-level efficient frontier DMUs, set $\mathbf{E}^1$.

Step 2: Exclude the frontier DMUs from future DEA runs. $\mathbf{J}^{l+1} = \mathbf{J}^l - \mathbf{E}^l$. (If $\mathbf{J}^{l+1} = \varnothing$ then stop.)

Step 3: Evaluate the new subset of "inefficient" DMUs, $\mathbf{J}^{l+1}$, by model (3.5) to obtain a new set of efficient DMUs $\mathbf{E}^{l+1}$ (the new efficient frontier).

Step 4: Let $l = l + 1$. Go to step 2.

Stopping rule: $\mathbf{J}^{l+1} = \varnothing$, the algorithm stops.

It can be seen that model (3.5) yields a stratification of the whole set of DMUs. From the algorithm, we know that l goes from 1 to L, where L is determined by the stopping rule. We have

1. $J^1 = \bigcup_{l=1}^{L} E^l$ and $E^l \cap E^{l'} = \varnothing$ for $l \neq l'$;
2. The DMUs in $E^{l'}$ are dominated by the DMUs in $E^{l'}$ if $l' > l$; and
3. Each DMU in set $E^{l'}$ is efficient with respect to the DMUs in set $E^{l+l'}$ for all $0 < l' \leq l - L$.

Note that in the above discussion, the input-oriented CRS envelopment model is used. The procedure remains unchanged if one uses the output-oriented CRS envelopment model, because the two models yield the same frontier, that is, the orientation of the models does not affect the identification of the efficient frontiers at different performance levels.

Note also that the above discussion can be applied to the VRS envelopment model where the identified frontiers exhibit VRS.

The *DEAFrontier* software has a Context-Dependent DEA menu item as shown in Figure 3.5. To obtain the efficient frontiers in different performance levels, we select the "Obtain Levels" which executes model (3.5) and its related algorithm. This prompts you to select a frontier type, as shown in Figure 3.6.

This function will first delete any sheet with a name starting with "Level" and then generate a set of new sheets named as "Level*i*(*Frontier*)" where *i* indicates the level and *Frontier* represents the frontier type. For example, Level1(VRS) means the first level VRS frontier. The "level" sheets are protected for use in the context-dependent DEA. However, they can be unprotected by using the "Unprotect the sheets" menu item. *The format of*

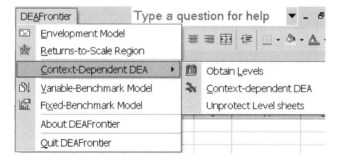

FIGURE 3.5 Context-Dependent DEA

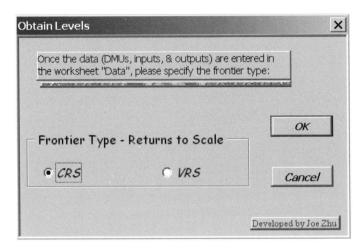

FIGURE 3.6   Obtain Efficient Frontiers

these level sheets must not be modified. Otherwise, the context-dependent DEA will not run properly and accurately.

Applying the CRS model to the CTAs in Table 2.1 yields five levels shown in Table 3.1. (see also the file CTA.xls in the CD.)

Input-Oriented Context-Dependent DEA

We now present the input-oriented context-dependent DEA based upon the evaluation context $E^l (l = 1, ..., L)$. The context-dependent DEA is characterized by an attractiveness measure and a progress measure.

TABLE 3.1   CTA Efficient Frontiers

Level	Efficient Frontier (Efficient CTAs)
1	CTA3, CTA4, CTA7
2	CTA2, CTA5, CTA6
3	CTA10, CTA11
4	CTA1
5	CTA8, CTA9

Consider a specific $DMU_q = (x_q, y_q)$ from a specific level $E^{l_o}, \in \{1, \ldots, L-1\}$. We use the following model to characterize the attractiveness.

$$H_q^*(d) = \min \ H_q(d) \qquad d = 1, \ldots, L - l_o$$

subject to

$$\sum_{j \in F(E^{l_o+d})} \lambda_j x_j \leq H_q(d) x_q$$

$$\sum_{j \in F(E^{l_o+d})} \lambda_j y_j \geq y_q \qquad\qquad (3.6)$$

$$\lambda_j \geq 0 \quad j \in F(E^{l_o+d})$$

Based upon Zhu (2003), we have for a specific $DMU_q \in E^{l_o}, l_o \in \{1, \ldots, L-1\}$, 1. $G_q^*(g) < 1$ for each $g = 1, \ldots, l_o - 1$ and 2. $H_q^*(d+1) > H_q^*(d)$. In model (3.6), each efficient frontier of E^{l_o+d} represents an evaluation context for measuring the relative attractiveness of DMUs in E^{l_o}. The larger the value of $H_q^*(d)$, the more attractive the DMU_q is. Because this DMU_q makes itself more distinctive from the evaluation context E^{l_o+d}. We are able to rank the DMUs in E^{l_o} based upon their attractiveness scores and identify the best one.

Definition 3.1 $H_q^*(d)$ is called (input-oriented) *d-degree* attractiveness of DMU_q from a specific level E^{l_o}.

Model (3.6) measures the relative attractiveness of DMUs in a selected level compared to efficient frontiers representing worse performance levels. Suppose, for example, each efficient DMU (in the first-level efficient frontier) represents a hedge fund, or CTA. We may compare a specific efficient DMU with other alternatives that are currently efficient (in the same level) as well as with relevant alternatives that serve as evaluation contexts. The relevant alternatives are those DMUs, say, in the second- or third-level efficient frontier, and so on. Given the alternatives (evaluation contexts), model (3.6) enables us to select the best option—the most attractive one.

If the efficient frontiers representing better performance levels are chosen as evaluation background, we obtain a measure of progress. For example, if the second-level efficient frontier is chosen as the evaluation background and we are to evaluate the DMUs in the third-level efficient frontier, we measure how much improvement or progress is expected for the third-level DMUs so that their performance can reach the second level.

The following linear programming problem is used to determine the progress score for

$$DMU_q \in E^{l_o}, \quad l_o \in \{2, \dots L\}.$$

$$G_q^*(g) = \min_{\lambda_j, G_q(g)} \ G_q(g) \qquad g = 1, \dots, l_o - 1$$

subject to

$$\sum_{j \in F(E^{l_o - g})} \lambda_j x_j \leq G_q(\beta) x_q$$

$$\sum_{j \in F(E^{l_o - g})} \lambda_j y_j \geq y_q \tag{3.7}$$

$$\lambda_j \geq 0 \quad j \in F(E^{l_o - g})$$

For a specific $DMU_q \in E^{l_o}$, $l_O \in \{2, \dots, L\}$, we have **1.** $G_q^*(g) < 1$ for each $g = 1, \dots, l_o - 1$, **2.** $G_q^*(g + 1) < G_q^*(g)$ (Zhu, 2003).

Definition 3.2 $M_q^*(g) \equiv 1/G_q^*(g)$ is called (input-oriented) *g-degree* progress of DMU_q from a specific level E^{l_o}.

Obviously $M_q^*(g) > 1$. For a larger $M_q^*(g)$, more progress is expected. Each efficient frontier, E^{l_o+g}, contains a possible target for a specific DMU in E^{l_o} to improve its performance. The progress here is a level-by-level improvement.

Output-Oriented Context-Dependent DEA

Similar to the discussion on the input-oriented context-dependent DEA, for a specific $DMU_q = (x_q, y_q)$ from a specific level E^{l_o}, $l_O \in \{1, \dots, L - 1\}$, we have the following model to characterize the output-oriented attractiveness:

$$\Omega_q^*(d) = \max_{\lambda_j, \Omega_q(d)} \ \Omega_q(d) \qquad d = 1, \dots, L - l_o$$

subject to

$$\sum_{j \in F(E^{l_o+d})} \lambda_j y_j \geq \Omega_q(d) y_q$$

$$\sum_{j \in F(E^{l_o+d})} \lambda_j x_j \leq x_q \tag{3.8}$$

$$\lambda_j \geq 0 \quad j \in F(E^{l_o+d})$$

For a specific $DMU_q \in E^{l_o}$, $l_o \in \{1, ..., L-1\}$, we have 1. $\Omega_q^*(d) < 1$ for each $d = 1, ..., L - l_o$ and 2. $\Omega_q^*(d+1) < \Omega_q^*(d)$.

Definition 3.3 $A_q^*(d) \equiv 1/\Omega_q^*(d)$ is called the (output-oriented) *d-degree* attractiveness of DMU_q from a specific level E^{l_o}.

Note that $A_q^*(d)$ is the reciprocal of the optimal value to (3.8), thus $A_q^*(d) > 1$. The larger the value of $A_q^*(d)$, the more attractive the DMU_q is. Because this DMU_q makes itself more distinctive from the evaluation context E^{l_o+d}.

The following linear programming problem determines the progress measure for $DMU_q \in E^{l_o}$, $l_o \in \{2, ..., L\}$.

$$P_q^*(g) = \max_{\lambda_j, P_q(g)} \ P_q(g) \qquad g = 1, ..., l_o - 1$$

subject to

$$\sum_{j \in F(E^{l_o - g})} \lambda_j y_j \geq P_q(g) y_q$$
$$\sum_{j \in F(E^{l_o - g})} \lambda_j x_j \leq x_q \qquad\qquad (3.9)$$
$$\lambda_j \geq 0 \quad j \in F(E^{l_o - g})$$

For a specific $DMU_q \in E^{l_o}$, $l_o \in \{2, ..., L\}$, we have 1. $P_q^*(g) > 1$ for each $g = 1, ..., l_o - 1$, and 2. $P_q^*(g+1) > P_q^*(g)$.

Definition 3.4 The optimal value to (3.9), that is, $P_q^*(g)$, is called the (output-oriented) *g-degree* progress of DMU_q from a specific level E^{l_o}.

For a larger $P_q^*(g)$, more progress is expected for DMU_q. Thus, a smaller value of $P_q^*(g)$ is preferred.

The above context-dependent DEA is based upon the CRS envelopment models. Similar models can be obtained under the condition of VRS where all efficient frontiers in different levels exhibit VRS, if we add $\sum \lambda_j = 1$ into the models (3.6) through (3.9). However, we should point out that the models for measuring attractiveness under the VRS condition may be infeasible. This is related to the infeasibility of a particular type of DEA model (see Seiford and Zhu, 1999b). The meaning of infeasibility is a subject for future studies. Therefore, we recommend that one uses the context-dependent DEA for the CRS condition, although the *DEAFrontier* software provides the context-dependent DEA for the VRS condition. However, we can still identify the VRS efficient frontiers in different performance levels.

Finally, the relationship between the input-oriented and output-oriented context-dependent DEA can be described as $H_q^*(d) = 1/\Omega_q^*(d)$, and $G_q^*(g) = 1/P_q^*(g)$. This indicates that the output-oriented attractiveness and progress measures can be obtained from the input-oriented context-dependent DEA. However, such relation is not necessarily true when the frontiers do not exhibit CRS.

Solving Context-Dependent DEA

Once different level efficient frontiers are identified, we use the "Context-Dependent DEA" menu item as shown in Figure 3.5. This prompts a dialog

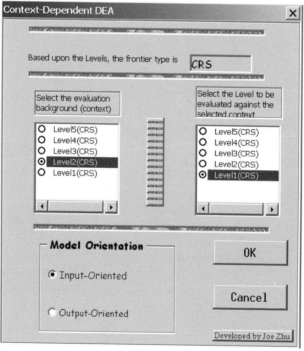

FIGURE 3.7   Solving Context-Dependent DEA

	A	B	C	D	E	F	G	H
1	Inputs		Outputs					
2	Standard Deviation		Monthly Return					
3	Proportion Negative		Skewness					
4			Minimum Return					
5								
6			*Input-Oriented*					
7			*Level2(CRS)*	Optimal Lambdas				
8	*DMU*	*Level1(CRS) DMU*	*Context-dependent Score*	with Benchmarks				
9	3	CTA3	1.38533	0.917 CTA2*			0.274 CTA6*	
10	4	CTA4	1.18230	1.418 CTA2*				
11	7	CTA7	1.17699	1.438 CTA5*				

FIGURE 3.8   Attractiveness

box as shown in Figure 3.6. It shows the type of frontier. In this case, it is CRS. In the left panel of Figure 3.7, we select the evaluation background—for example, level-2 efficient frontier. In the right panel, we select the level under evaluation, for example, level 1. In this case, we are interested in the (first degree) attractiveness for the CRS efficient CTAs.

The results are reported in the "Context-Dependent Result" sheet (Figure 3.8). In this sheet, the context-dependent scores are the optimal values to models (3.6) through (3.9). To obtain the attractiveness or progress scores, one has to adjust the context-dependent scores based upon Definitions 3.2 through 3.5.

Figure 3.8 shows the results. Column A reports the DMU number, and Column B reports the DMUs being evaluated. Column C reports the optimal value to model (3.6) when level 1 is compared to the level-2 efficient frontier. In this case, the optimal value or the context-dependent score is the attractiveness score based upon definition 3.1. It can be seen that CTA3 has the highest score and therefore is the most attractive one. The result sheet also reports the non-zero optimal λ_j^*, indicating which DMUs are served as benchmarks. For example, Figure 3.8 indicates that CTA2 and CTA6 are used as benchmarks when CTA3 is evaluated against the level-2 efficient frontier.

If we change the evaluation background to the third-level CRS frontier, including CTAs 10 and 11, we measure the second-degree attractiveness. This is achieved by selecting the third-level CRS frontier in Figure 3.6. Based upon the attractiveness scores shown in Figure 3.9, CTA7 becomes

	A	B	C	D	E
1	Inputs		Outputs		
2	Standard Deviation		Monthly Return		
3	Proportion Negative		Skewness		
4			Minimum Return		
5					
6			Input-Oriented		
7			Level3(CRS)	Optimal Lambdas	
8	DMU No.	Level1(CRS) DMU Name	Context-dependent Score	with Benchmarks	
9	3	CTA3	1.67632	1.140 CTA10	
10	4	CTA4	1.30097	1.194 CTA10	
11	7	CTA7	2.00261	1.683 CTA10	

FIGURE 3.9   Second-Degree Attractiveness

the most attractive one. This example illustrates that under a different evaluation context, the attractiveness of DMUs on the same level may be different. Therefore, the context-dependent DEA differentiates the performance of efficient DMUs, or DMUs on the same performance level.

CHAPTER 4

Benchmarking Models

INTRODUCTION

Benchmarking is a process of defining valid measures of performance comparison among peer entities (DMUs), using them to determine the relative positions of the peer DMUs, and, ultimately, establishing a standard of excellence. In that sense, DEA can be regarded as a benchmarking tool, because the frontier identified can be regarded as an empirical standard of excellence. Once the frontier is established, we may compare a set of new DMUs to the frontier. However, when a new DMU outperforms the identified frontier, a new frontier is generated by DEA. As a result, we do not have the same benchmark (frontier) for other (new) DMUs.

In this chapter, we present a number of DEA-based benchmarking models where each (new) DMU is evaluated against a set of given benchmarks (standards).

VARIABLE-BENCHMARK MODEL

Let E^* represent the set of benchmarks or the best-practice identified by the DEA. Based upon the input-oriented CRS envelopment model, we have

$$\min \delta^{CRS}$$

subject to

$$\sum_{j \in E^*} \lambda_j x_{ij} \leq \delta^{CRS} x_i^{new}$$

$$\sum_{j \in E^*} \lambda_j y_{rj} \geq y_r^{new} \qquad (4.1)$$

$$\lambda_j \geq 0, j \in E^*$$

where a new observation is represented by DMU^{new} with inputs x_i^{new} ($i = 1, \ldots, m$) and outputs y_r^{new} ($r = 1, \ldots, s$). The superscript of CRS indicates that the benchmark frontier composed by benchmark DMUs in set E^* exhibits CRS.

Model (4.1) measures the performance of DMU^{new} with respect to benchmark DMUs in set E^* when outputs are fixed at their current levels. Similarly, based upon the output-oriented CRS envelopment model, we can have a model that measures the performance of DMU^{new} in terms of outputs when inputs are fixed at their current levels.

$$\max \ \tau^{CRS}$$

subject to

$$\sum_{j \in E^*} \lambda_j x_{ij} \le x_i^{new}$$

$$\sum_{j \in E^*} \lambda_j y_{rj} \ge t^{CRS} y_r^{neu} \tag{4.2}$$

$$\lambda_j \ge 0, j \in E^*$$

Theorem 4.1

$\delta^{CRS*} = 1/\tau^{CRS*}$, where δ^{CRS*} is the optimal value to model (4.1) and τ_0^{CRS*} is the optimal value to model (4.2).

Proof: Suppose $\lambda_j^*(j \in E^*)$ is an optimal solution associated with δ^{CRS*} in model (4.1). Now, let $\tau^{CRS*} = 1/\delta^{CRS*}$, and $\lambda_j' = \lambda_j^* \delta_0^{CRS*}$. Then τ^{CRS*} and λ_j' are optimal in model (4.2). Thus, $\delta^{CRS*} = 1/\tau^{CRS*}$.

Model (4.1) or (4.2) yields a benchmark for DMU^{new}. The ith input and the rth output for the benchmark can be expressed as

$$\begin{cases} \displaystyle\sum_{j \in E^*} \lambda_j^* x_{ij} & (i\text{th input}) \\ \displaystyle\sum_{j \in E^*} \lambda_j^* y_{ij} & (r\text{th output}) \end{cases} \tag{4.3}$$

Note also that although the DMUs associated with set E^* are given, the resulting benchmark may be different for each new DMU under evaluation. For each new DMU under evaluation, (4.3) may represent a different combination of DMUs associated with set E^*. Thus, models (4.1) and (4.2) represent a variable-benchmark scenario.

Theorem 4.2

1. $\delta^{CRS*} < 1$ or $\tau^{CRS*} > 1$ indicates that the performance of DMU^{new} is dominated by the benchmark in (4.3).
2. $\delta^{CRS*} = 1$ or $\tau^{CRS*} = 1$ indicates that DMU^{new} achieves the same performance level of the benchmark in (4.3).
3. $\delta^{CRS*} > 1$ or $\tau^{CRS*} < 1$ indicates that input savings or output surpluses exist in DMU^{new} when compared to the benchmark in (4.3).

Proof: 1. and 2. are obvious results in terms of DEA efficiency concept. Now, $\delta^{CRS*} > 1$ indicates that DMU^{new} can increase its inputs to reach the benchmark. This in turn indicates that $\delta^{CRS*} - 1$ measures the input saving achieved by DMU^{new}. Similarly, $\tau^{CRS*} < 1$ indicates that DMU^{new} can decrease its outputs to reach the benchmark. This in turn indicates that $1 - \tau^{CRS*}$ measures the output surplus achieved by DMU^{new}.

Figure 4.1 illustrates the three cases described in Theorem 4.2. ABC ($A'B'C'$) represents the input (output) benchmark frontier. D, H and G (or D', H', and G') represent the new DMUs to be benchmarked against ABC (or $A'B'C'$). We have $\delta_D^{CRS*} > 1$ for DMU D ($\tau_{D'}^{CRS*} < 1$ for DMU D') indicating that DMU D can increase its input values by δ_D^{CRS*} while producing the same amount of outputs generated by the benchmark (DMU D' can decrease its output levels while using the same amount of input levels consumed by the benchmark). Thus, $\delta_D^{CRS*} > 1$ is a measure of input savings achieved by DMU D and $\tau_{D'}^{CRS*} < 1$ is a measure of output surpluses achieved by DMU D'.

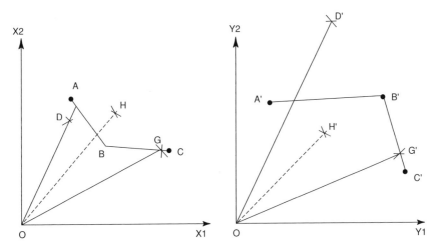

FIGURE 4.1 Variable-Benchmark Model

For DMU G and DMU G', we have $\delta_G^{CRS*} = 1$ and $\tau_{G'}^{CRS*} = 1$, indicating that they achieve the same performance level of the benchmark and no input savings or output surpluses exist. For DMU H and DMU H', we have $\delta_H^{CRS*} < 1$ and $\tau_{H'}^{CRS*} > 1$, indicating that inefficiency exists in the performance of these two DMUs.

Note that for example, in Figure 4.1, a convex combination of DMU A and DMU B is used as the benchmark for DMU D, while a convex combination of DMU B and DMU C is used as the benchmark for DMU G. Thus, models (4.1) and (4.2) are called variable-benchmark models.

From Theorem 4.2, we can define $\delta^{CRS*} - 1$ or $1 - \tau^{CRS*}$ as the performance gap between DMU^{new} and the benchmark. Based upon δ^{CRS*} or τ^{CRS*}, a ranking of the benchmarking performance can be obtained.

It is likely that scale inefficiency may be allowed in the benchmarking. We therefore modify models (4.1) and (4.2) to incorporate scale inefficiency by assuming VRS.

min δ^{VRS}
          subject to

$$\sum_{j \in E^*} \lambda_j x_{ij} \leq \delta^{VRS} x_i^{new}$$

$$\sum_{j \in E^*} \lambda_j y_{rj} \geq y_r^{new}$$

$$\sum_{j \in E^*} \lambda_j = 1 \qquad\qquad (4.4)$$

$$\lambda_j \geq 0, j \in E^*$$

max τ^{VRS}
          subject to

$$\sum_{j \in E^*} \lambda_j x_{ij} \leq x_i^{new}$$

$$\sum_{j \in E^*} \lambda_j y_{rj} \geq \tau^{VRS} y_r^{new}$$

$$\sum_{j \in E^*} \lambda_j = 1 \qquad\qquad (4.5)$$

$$\lambda_j \geq 0, j \in E^*$$

Similar to Theorem 4.2, we have

Theorem 4.3

1. $\delta^{VRS*} < 1$ or $\tau^{VRS*} > 1$ indicates that the performance of DMU^{new} is dominated by the benchmark in (4.3).
2. $\delta^{VRS*} = 1$ or $\tau^{VRS*} = 1$ indicates that DMU^{new} achieves the same performance level of the benchmark in (4.3).
3. $\delta^{VRS*} > 1$ or $\tau^{VRS*} < 1$ indicates that input savings or output surpluses exist in DMU^{new} when compared to the benchmark in (4.3).

Note that model (4.2) is always feasible, and model (4.1) is infeasible only if certain patterns of zero data are present (Zhu 1996). Thus, if we assume that all the data are positive, (4.1) is always feasible. However, unlike models (4.1) and (4.2), models (4.4) and (4.5) may be infeasible. Based upon the necessary and sufficient conditions for infeasibility in super-efficiency DEA models provided in Seiford and Zhu (1999b), we have

Theorem 4.4

1. If model (4.4) is infeasible, then the output vector of DMU^{new} dominates the output vector of the benchmark in (4.3).
2. If model (4.5) is infeasible, then the input vector of DMU^{new} dominates the input vector of the benchmark in (4.3).

The implication of the infeasibility associated with models (4.4) and (4.5) needs to be carefully examined. Consider Figure 4.2 where ABC represents

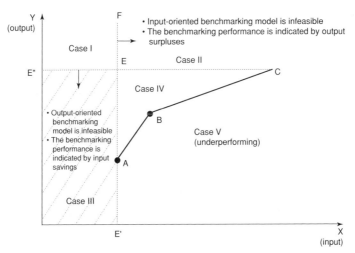

FIGURE 4.2 Infeasibility of VRS Variable-Benchmark Model

the benchmark frontier. Models (4.4) and (4.5) yield finite optimal values for any DMU^{new} located below EC and to the right of EA. Model (4.4) is infeasible for DMU^{new} located above ray $E''C$ and model (4.5) is infeasible for DMU^{new} located to the left of ray $E'E$.

Both models (4.4) and (4.5) are infeasible for DMU^{new} located above $E''E$ and to the left of ray EF. Note that if DMU^{new} is located above $E''C$, its output value is greater than the output value of any convex combinations of A, B and C.

Note also that if DMU^{new} is located to the left of $E'F$, its input value is less than the input value of any convex combinations of A, B, and C.

Based upon Theorem 4.4 and Figure 4.2, we have four cases:

Case I: When both models (4.4) and (4.5) are infeasible, this indicates that DMU^{new} has the smallest input level and the largest output level compared to the benchmark. Thus, both input savings and output surpluses exist in DMU^{new}.

Case II: When model (4.4) is infeasible and model (4.5) is feasible, the infeasibility of model (4.4) is caused by the fact that DMU^{new} has the largest output level compared to the benchmark. Thus, we use model (4.5) to characterize the output surpluses.

Case III: When model (4.5) is infeasible and model (4.4) is feasible, the infeasibility of model (4.5) is caused by the fact that DMU^{new} has the smallest input level compared to the benchmark. Thus, we use model (4.4) to characterize the input savings.

Case IV: When both models (4.4) and (4.5) are feasible, we use them to determine whether input savings and output surpluses exist.

SOLVING VARIABLE-BENCHMARK MODEL

To solve the variable-benchmark model, one needs to set up two sheets containing the data. For example, consider the 11 CTAs shown in Figure 2.7. Suppose we choose CTA7 with the highest monthly return as the benchmark. This benchmark is entered in a sheet named "benchmarks." The remaining CTAs are to be evaluated against this benchmark and entered in the sheet named "DMUs." The "benchmarks" and "DMUs" sheets have the same format requirement as shown in Figure 2.7. We then select the "Variable-Benchmark Model" menu item as shown in Figure 4.3 and make the model selection as shown in Figure 4.4. In this case, we use the default selection of input-oriented CRS variable-benchmark model. The results are reported in a sheet named "Benchmarking results," as shown in Figure 4.5. The benchmarking score in column C gives a ranking of the remaining 10 CTAs. A higher score indicates a better performance with respect to the selected inputs and outputs.

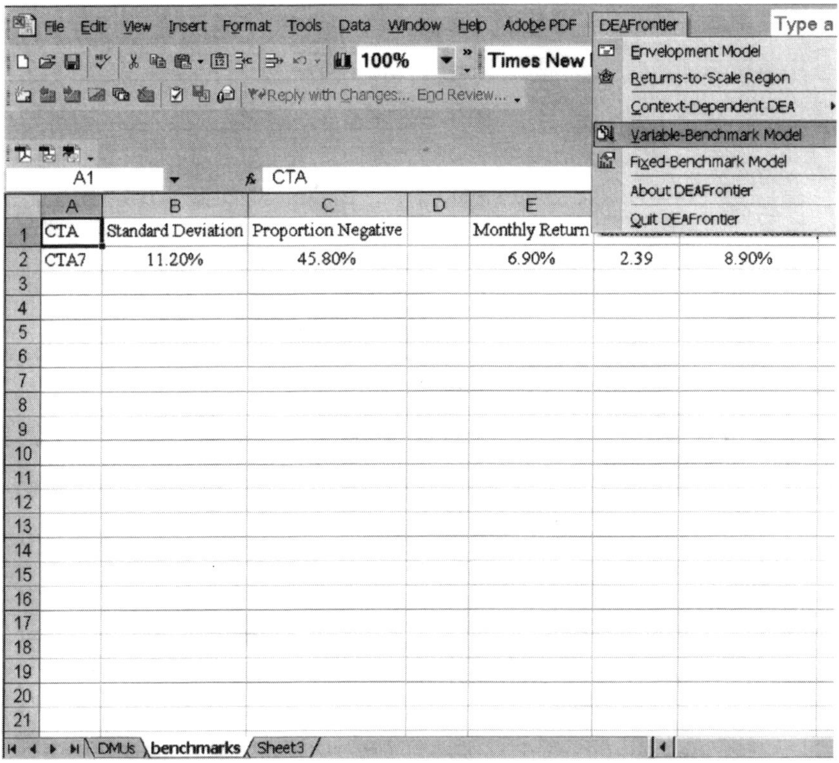

FIGURE 4.3 Solving Variable-Benchmark Model

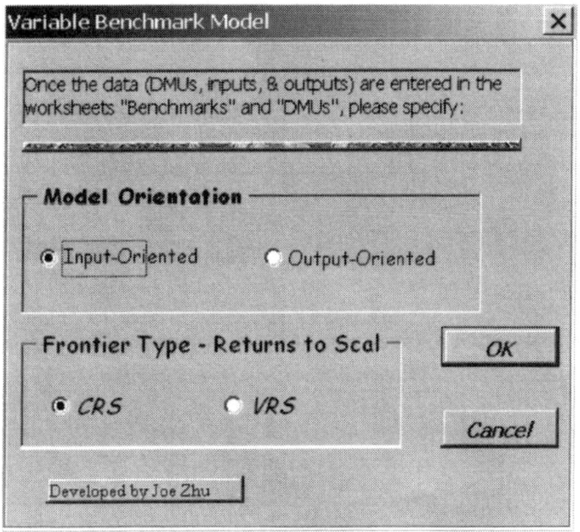

FIGURE 4.4 Variable-Benchmark Model Selection

	A	B	C	D	E
1	Inputs		Outputs		
2	Standard Deviation		Monthly Return		
3	Proportion Negative		Skewness		
4			Minimum Return		
5					
6			Input-Oriented		
7			CRS		
8	DMU No.	New DMU Name	Benchmark Score	Benchmarks	
9	1	CTA1	3.31262	2.011 CTA7	
10	2	CTA2	5.69438	2.034 CTA7	
11	3	CTA3	8.14276	2.472 CTA7	
12	4	CTA4	5.13438	2.292 CTA7	
13	5	CTA5	4.76596	2.000 CTA7	
14	6	CTA6	6.52395	2.213 CTA7	
15	7	CTA8	0.90063	1.029 CTA7	
16	8	CTA9	1.33333	1.000 CTA7	
17	9	CTA10	4.85753	2.169 CTA7	
18	10	CTA11	1.95551	1.067 CTA7	
19					
20					
21					

H ◀ ▶ H \ Benchmarking Result / DMUs / benchmarks / Sheet3 /

FIGURE 4.5 Benchmarking Results

FIXED-BENCHMARK MODEL

Although the benchmark frontier is given in the variable-benchmark models, a DMU^{new} under benchmarking has the freedom to choose a subset of benchmarks so that the performance of DMU^{new} can be characterized in the most favorable light. Situations when the same benchmark should be fixed are likely to occur. For example, the management may indicate that DMUs A and B in Figure 4.1 should be used as the fixed benchmark, that is, DMU C in Figure 4.1 may not be used in constructing the benchmark.

To deal with this situation, we turn to the multiplier models (the dual models to the envelopment models). For example, the input-oriented CRS multiplier model determines a set of referent best-practice DMUs represented by a set of binding constraints in optimality.

Let set $B = \{DMU_j : j \in \mathbf{I}_B\}$ be the selected subset of benchmark set E^*, that is, $\mathbf{I}_B \subset E^*$. Based upon the input-oriented CRS multiplier model, we have

$$\tilde{\sigma}^{CRS*} = \max \sum_{r=1}^{s} \mu_r y_r^{new}$$

subject to

$$\sum_{r=1}^{s} \mu_r y_{rj} - \sum_{i=1}^{s} v_i x_{ij} = 0 \quad j \in \mathbf{I}_B$$

$$\sum_{r=1}^{s} \mu_r y_{rj} - \sum_{i=1}^{s} v_i x_{ij} \leq 0 \quad j \notin \mathbf{I}_B$$

$$\sum_{i=1}^{m} v_i x_i^{new} = 1$$

$$\mu_r, v_i \geq 0.$$

(4.6)

TABLE 4.1   Fixed-Benchmark Models

Frontier Type	Input-Oriented	Output-Oriented
	$\max \sum_{r=1}^{s} \mu_r y_r^{new} + \mu$	$\min \sum_{i=1}^{m} v_i x_i^{new} + v$
	subject to	subject to
	$\sum_{r=1}^{s} \mu_r y_{rj} - \sum_{i=1}^{s} v_i x_{ij} + \mu = 0 \quad j \in \mathbf{I}_B$	$\sum_{i=1}^{s} v_i x_{ij} - \sum_{r=1}^{s} \mu_r y_{rj} + v = 0 \quad j \in \mathbf{I}_B$
	$\sum_{r=1}^{s} \mu_r y_{rj} - \sum_{i=1}^{s} v_i x_{ij} + \mu \le 0 \quad j \notin \mathbf{I}_B$	$\sum_{i=1}^{s} v_i x_{ij} - \sum_{r=1}^{s} \mu_r y_{rj} + v \ge 0 \quad j \notin \mathbf{I}_B$
	$\sum_{i=1}^{m} v_i x_i^{new} = 1$	$\sum_{r=1}^{s} \mu_r y_r^{new} = 1$
	$\mu_r, v_i \ge 0$	$\mu_r, v_i \ge 0$
CRS	where $\mu = 0$	where $v = 0$
VRS	where μ free	where v free

By applying equalities in the constraints associated with benchmark DMUs, model (4.6) measures DMU^{new}'s performance against the benchmark constructed by set **B**. At optimality, some DMU_j $j \notin \mathbf{I}_B$ may join the fixed-benchmark set if the associated constraints are binding.

Note that model (4.6) may be infeasible. For example, the DMUs in set **B** may not be fit into the same facet when they number greater than m + s −1, where *m* is the number of inputs and *s* is the number of outputs. In this case, we need to adjust the set **B**.

Three possible cases are associated with model (4.6). $\tilde{\sigma}^{CRS*} > 1$ indicating that DMU^{new} outperforms the benchmark. $\tilde{\sigma}^{CRS*} = 1$ indicating that DMU^{new} achieves the same performance level of the benchmark. $\tilde{\sigma}^{CRS*} < 1$ indicating that the benchmark outperforms DMU^{new}.

By applying RTS frontier type and model orientation, we obtain the fixed-benchmark models in Table 4.1.

DMU^{new} is not included in the constraints of

$$\sum_{r=1}^{s} \mu_r y_{rj} - \sum_{i=1}^{m} v_i x_{ij} + \mu < 0 \; (j \notin \mathbf{I}_B)$$

$$\left(\sum_{i=1}^{m} v_i x_{ij} - \sum_{r=1}^{s} \mu_r y_{rj} + v \ge 0 \; (j \notin \mathbf{I}_B) \right)$$

However, other peer DMUs $(j \notin \mathbf{I}_B)$ are included.

SOLVING FIXED-BENCHMARK MODEL

To solve the fixed-benchmark models, one needs to set up two data sheets, namely "Benchmarks" and "DMUs." Then select the "Fixed-Benchmark Model" menu item in Figure 4.3. A window similar to Figure 4.4 for model selection will be displayed. The results are reported in a sheet named "Efficiency Report."

CHAPTER 5

Data, Inputs, and Outputs

DESCRIPTION OF DATA

The data set for the models in the application chapters is the 20 largest live hedge funds, funds of hedge funds, and CTAs in terms of ending assets under management. However, some classifications have less than 20 funds during the examination period. The data come from the Centre for International Securities and Derivatives Markets (CISDM) databases, and cover monthly returns net of all management and performance fees from January 1998 to June 2004. We use this period because it covers the extreme market events of August 1998, as well as the September 11, 2001, terrorist attacks. Using a longer time frame would have resulted in fewer funds per classification and yielded less-than-optimal results.

The top 20 hedge funds, FOFs and CTAs from each category are used because past studies have demonstrated that they tend to survive longer (Gregoriou, 2002; Gregoriou, 2003; Gregoriou, Hubner, Papageorgiou, and Rouah, 2004). As these authors note, survivorship bias is almost nonexistent when using large funds, but is significant in small funds (<$50 million). Therefore, smaller hedge funds and smaller CTAs (<$50 million) have the largest presence in both dead hedge fund and CTA CISDM databases. Additionally, many small hedge funds or CTAs that do not perform well in their first year find it difficult to collect performance fees, which in turn makes it difficult to maintain their organizational structure and operations.

The CISDM database separates CTAs and hedge funds into five and ten classifications, respectively. We present short definitions of each in Tables 5.1 and 5.2. The agricultural, long-only, and short-seller classifications contain only a handful of funds; this may result in all the funds being rated as

TABLE 5.1 Definition of Commodity Trading Advisor Classifications

Classifications	Definition of Investment Style
Diversified	Manager trades financial futures/options, currency futures/options, and forward contracts as well as commodity futures/options. Manager limits risk by holding a large number of positions.
Currency	Manager trades currency futures/options, forward contracts, and specializes in currency trading.
Financial	Manager trades financial futures/options as well as currency futures/options, forward contracts and currency, interest rate, stock indexes, and precious metals.
Agricultural	Manager specializes in agricultural futures options trading.
Stock Index	Manager specializes in stock index futures and options.

Source: Schneeweis, T. [2003] IDAC. Reprinted with permission of CISDM.

efficient. To correct for this, we reduce the number of inputs to one and the number of outputs to two.

We provide monthly summary statistics in Table 5.3 and Table 5.4 to better understand the risk and return associated with each style classification. The Sharpe ratio, developed by Nobel Laureate William F. Sharpe of Stanford University, is a risk-adjusted measure calculated by subtracting the risk-free rate from the portfolio return (excess return), and then dividing by the standard deviation of returns. In other words, the higher the Sharpe ratio, the better the fund's performance. This well-known ratio is likely to be the highest for FOFs (a basket of various hedge funds with different strategies) and non-directional funds (event-driven and market-neutral). The latter two classifications do not rely on any type of market movement and usually take advantage of market inefficiencies. Furthermore, the average standard deviation is usually lower for non-directional funds because they are not exposed to market risk. Directional funds generally profit from the direction of the market and follow various global trends.

A drawback of using hedge funds, however, is that they tend to produce negative skewness. During the investigation period, we note that CTAs display positive skewness, which makes them attractive stand-alone diversifiers for traditional stock and bond portfolios. This may be explained by the negative correlation they possess with respect to traditional stock and bond market indices. From January 1998 to June 2004, the S&P 500 index returned a paltry 29.26%, but the average CTA returned 48.23%. We find that CTAs produce lower standard deviation, positive skewness, and lower kurtosis than hedge funds during our sample period (see Tables 5.3 and 5.4).

TABLE 5.2 Definition of Hedge Fund Classifications

Classification	Definition of Investment Style
Panel A. Directional	
Global International	Manager pays attention to economic changes around the world (except in the United States).
Global Macro	Opportunistic trading manager profits from changes in global economies, typically based on major interest rate shifts.
Short Sellers	Manager takes a position that stock prices will go down. Used as a hedge for short-only portfolios.
Long-Only	Manager takes a position that stock prices will go up.
Global Emerging	Manager invests in less mature financial markets. Because shorting is not permitted in many emerging markets, managers must go to cash or other markets when evaluations make being long unattractive.
Global Established	Manager focuses on opportunities in established markets such as the United States, Europe, and Japan.
Sector	Manager follows specific economic sectors and/or industries and can use a wide range of methodologies.
Panel B. Non-Directional	
Market-Neutral	Manager goes half-long/half-short and attempts to lock out or neutralize risk.
Event-Driven	Manager focuses on securities of companies in reorganization and bankruptcy, ranging from senior-secured debt to common stock.
Panel C. Neither Directional nor Non-Directional	
Fund of Hedge Funds	Manager allocates capital among a number of hedge funds.

Source: Ackermann et al., *Journal of Finance* (1999). Reproduced with permission of Blackwell Pubs (J) (Legacy) in the format trade book via Copyright Clearance Center. © 1999 by Blackwell Pubs.

Hedge fund and CTA returns do not follow normal distributions (Fung and Hsieh, 1997). The distribution of their returns are asymmetrical and display fatter tails then the normal distribution (see Tables 5.3 and 5.4). Non-directional strategies display fatter tails (excess kurtosis) and possess lower volatility than directional strategies, a finding confirmed by Kouwenberg (2003) using ZCM data from 1995 to 2001. He observed that non-directional classifications had the most prominent non-normality and possessed

TABLE 5.3 Monthly Summary Statistics for Hedge Fund Classifications (January 1998 through June 2004)

	Monthly Average Return	Monthly Average Standard Deviation	Monthly Skewness	Monthly Kurtosis	Monthly Average Traditional Sharpe
Fund of Hedge Funds	0.80	1.96	−0.64	5.81	0.25
Event-Driven	0.95	2.04	−0.70	6.43	0.30
Market-Neutral	0.86	2.01	−1.76	12.93	0.26
Global Macro	1.21	3.93	0.34	3.53	0.21
Global International	1.31	5.56	0.09	2.43	0.17
Global Emerging	1.55	8.30	−0.78	10.42	0.15
Global Established	1.33	4.16	0.65	4.46	0.23
Short Sellers	1.00	9.79	−0.14	4.41	0.08
Long-Only	1.61	9.23	0.36	6.27	0.12
Sector	1.48	6.56	0.49	2.29	0.18

the highest kurtosis, which indicates a high probability of a loss or gain and the largest negative skewness.

High kurtosis implies more returns close to the mean with more frequent large positive or negative returns than a normal distribution of returns. This signifies a high probability that extreme market events will occur. One reason may be that non-directional strategies possess payoffs like short option strategies, while directional strategies possess long-only

TABLE 5.4 Monthly Summary Statistics for CTA Classifications (January 1998 through June 2004)

	Monthly Average Return	Monthly Average Standard Deviation	Monthly Skewness	Monthly Kurtosis	Monthly Average Traditional Sharpe
Diversified	0.90	4.50	0.38	2.34	0.34
Financials	0.76	4.94	0.55	1.69	0.21
Currency	0.59	3.44	0.84	2.39	0.11
Stock Index	1.27	5.30	0.13	2.47	0.34
Agricultural	0.89	4.34	0.48	2.26	0.26

option strategies (for example, hedge fund managers invest in the markets by using quantitative or fundamental models or private information, and try to benefit from the upside of the market as well as from the downside).

Furthermore, we notice that non-directional funds (event-driven and market-neutral) have a low standard deviation and high excess kurtosis, while directional (market-timing) funds—such as global macro, global international, global emerging, global established, and sector—display a high standard deviation with low excess kurtosis given their greater exposure to market risk.

METHODOLOGY

Since there is no standard agreement from past hedge fund and CTA studies regarding inputs and outputs used (Gregoriou, Sedzro, and Zhu, 2005; Gregoriou, 2003; Gregoriou, Rouah, Satchell, and Diz, in press), we explain why we selected two inputs and five outputs. In the DEA literature, it is generally accepted that the sample should be two times larger than the sum of the inputs and outputs used in the analysis. In each of our DEA models we use a different number of outputs for diversity and keep the same number of inputs. This does not mean using other inputs or outputs is incorrect; the selection is at the discretion of the investor.

In DEA, an efficiency score of 1.0 (100%) signifies that a hedge fund or CTA is efficient, and that no other fund has produced better outputs with the inputs used for an input-oriented model. When using output-oriented models, a lower efficiency score is considered more efficient. However, it does not imply that all funds with a score of 1.0 provided the same return during the examination period, just that the return is the maximum for the incurred risk. In addition, note that the efficiency score is not absolute. A fund with an efficiency score of 1.0 (100%) returning 20% is considered more risky than a fund with a score of 1.0 (100%) returning 15%. We use an input orientation for three models, and a combination of both for the remaining. When using input-oriented context-dependent, fixed- and variable-benchmark models, the higher the score the greater the efficiency. Scores in these models can be greater than one and the reverse applies for output-oriented models.

Inputs

An input is simply any resource used by a fund to produce its outputs. We use two inputs, the first being (1) *monthly average standard deviation* as a measure of investment risk, because it captures the variability of normal returns. A small standard deviation represents a low probability of extraordinary gains or losses; a large standard deviation implies a high probability of extraordinary gains or losses. The scale of the standard deviation can indicate the level of a fund's risk, and specify which funds are more efficient at controlling for or minimizing standard deviation.

We follow this with (2) *monthly loss deviation*, which calculates the average mean return for only the periods with a loss and then measures the variation of only the losing periods around this loss mean. This statistic is used to measure the volatility of downside performance to, in essence, minimize loss deviation. By doing so, the exposure to hedge funds and CTA stocks that possess a higher probability of negative returns is reduced. Smaller inputs and larger outputs in DEA usually indicate better performance.

Outputs

Outputs are the result of the processing of inputs, and can measure how efficiently a hedge fund or CTA has attained its goals. We use the following five outputs:

1. monthly average return
2. monthly average gain
3. monthly percent profitable
4. annualized monthly compounded return
5. maximum consecutive gain

Monthly average return is calculated by adding the monthly return and dividing by the number of periods. Since this is an average measure encompassing the average of both positive and negative returns, we select and isolate the monthly average gain (this is the arithmetic mean of the monthly periods with a gain during the period calculated by adding the gain period returns and then dividing by the number of gain monthly periods). This identifies funds that have attained the largest average monthly gains and can be used as a measure of consistency for producing positive returns. Annualized monthly compound return is the constant annual return that results in the same compound return as the series over the examination period.

Monthly percent profitable refers to the number of positive months divided by the total number of months. This identifies funds that are efficient in producing and sustaining the greatest number of positive months throughout this turbulent period. Finally, the maximum consecutive gain is simply the number of consecutive months the fund has attained positive returns during the investigation period. This output identifies efficient funds that are able to maintain a superior level of performance persistence during the period.

As we noted earlier, we use two inputs and five outputs for the VRS model, but for the remaining models we use a subset of the inputs and out-

TABLE 5.5 Inputs and Outputs for Each Model

DEA Models	Inputs	Outputs
VRS, CRS	Average Standard Deviation, Average Loss Deviation	Average Monthly Gain, Average Monthly Return, Monthly Percent Profitable, Annualized Monthly Compound Return, Maximum Consecutive Gain
RTS	Average Standard Deviation, Average Loss Deviation	Monthly Percent Profitable, Annualized Monthly Compound Return, Maximum Consecutive Gain
Context-Dependent	Average Standard Deviation, Average Loss Deviation	Monthly Average Gain, Maximum Consecutive Gain, and Compound Return
Fixed- and Variable-Benchmark Models	Average Standard Deviation, Average Loss Deviation	Average Monthly Gain, Average Monthly Return, Monthly Percent Profitable, Annualized Monthly Compound Return, Maximum Consecutive Gain

puts outlined in Table 5.5. For classifications with a handful of funds, one input (average loss deviation) and two outputs (average monthly gain and compound return) are used in the various models.

PREPARING THE DATA FOR DEAFrontier

To begin, open a new Excel spreadsheet. From the toolbar select Tools then click on Solver. This brings up the solver parameters box. Once the solver parameters box appears, it can then be closed. Now the solver has been invoked. From the file menu, select open and then double click on *DEAFrontier*. You will then click on enable macros and DEA will appear in the toolbar. At the bottom left of the spreadsheet you must rename Sheet 1 to Data. For the VRS and CRS (Envelopment Model), Returns-to-Scale Region and Context-Dependent models the data can be copied and pasted in the Data spreadsheet. The first column must contain the name of the funds, while the second and third columns are for inputs (more columns can be added if more inputs are used). A blank column must always separate the inputs and outputs. After the blank column, the first output can be added, then the second, and so on.

Type a question for help

DEAFronter

- Envelopment Model
- Returns-to-Scale Region
- Context-Dependent DEA
- Variable-Benchmark Model
- Fixed-Benchmark Model
- About DEAFrontier
- Quit DEAFrontier

	A	B	C	D	E	F			I
1	FOF NAME	AV STD DEV	AV LOSS DEV		MTH AV RET	MTH AV			X CONS GAIN
2	GAM DIVERSITY FUND	0.025	0.021		0.0087	0.018	0.7852	0.1052	0.4751
3	PERMAL INVESTMENT HOLDINGS NV (A)	0.0359	0.0296		0.0069	0.0261	0.6154	0.0777	0.4861
4	HAUSSMAN HOLDINGS NV	0.0296	0.0202		0.0055	0.0232	0.5641	0.063	0.3
5	MESIROW ALTERNATIVE STRATEGIES FUND	0.0112	0.0178		0.0062	0.0093	0.859	0.0765	0.3037
6	JP MORGAN MULTI-STRATEGY FUND	0.0023	0.0106		0.0081	0.0122	0.8077	0.1013	0.5877
7	MAN-GLENWOOD MULTI-STRATEGY FUND	0.0151	0.0127		0.0047	0.0107	0.7436	0.057	0.3289
8	COAST DIVERSIFIED FUND	0.0106	0.01		0.0094	0.0117	0.8462	0.1052	0.5376
9	AURORA	0.0142	0.0086		0.0082	0.0124	0.8333	0.1013	0.5144
10	LIGHTHOUSE DIVERSIFIED FUND	0.0118	0.0125		0.0079	0.011	0.8462	0.0983	0.4583
11	MESIROW EQUITY OPPORTUNITY FUND	0.0141	0.0089		0.0083	0.0134	0.7564	0.1024	0.1969
12	MERIDIAN HORIZON FUND	0.0179	0.0131		0.0104	0.0155	0.7821	0.13	0.4343
13	LEVERAGED CAPITAL HOLDINGS	0.0354	0.0266		0.0057	0.0271	0.5513	0.0624	0.2328
14	IRONWOOD PARTNERS	0.0102	0.0087		0.0093	0.0113	0.9103	0.1163	0.6611
15	MESIROW EVENT STRATEGIES FUND	0.0113	0.0076		0.0083	0.011	0.9103	0.1074	0.4097
16	MOMENTUM ALL WEATHER FUND	0.01	0.0189		0.0086	0.0077	0.8846	0.069	0.2676
17	GREEN WAY CLASS B (EURO)	0.0143	0.0055		0.0056	0.0108	0.7051	0.0568	0.1101
18	PERMAL JAPAN HOLDINGS	0.0376	0.0133		0.0047	0.0314	0.6154	0.1104	0.583
19	ASIAN CAPITAL HOLDINGS FUND	0.0427	0.0202		0.0181	0.0377	0.5256	0.0848	0.3989
20	EDISON FUND CLASS A	0.0239	0.0028		0.0094	0.0249	0.8462	0.236	0.6831
21	DKR INTL RELATIVE VALUE (A)	0.0083	0.0045		0.0077	0.004	0.859	0.1045	0.4586

Data

Figure 5.1   Screen Shot of the Data Sheet

Once the screenshot is set up as in Figure 5.1, click on *DEAFrontier* in the drop-down box, and five models will appear:

1. envelopment
2. returns-to-scale region
3. context-dependent DEA
4. variable-benchmark model
5. fixed-benchmark model

For example, if you select "envelopment model," you must next decide on the model orientation you require (an input- or output-oriented model). Then you must select either CRS or VRS, click "OK," and the efficiency scores will be generated in a new spreadsheet under a tab called Efficiency.

If you select the fixed- and variable-benchmark models, you must create a new spreadsheet and rename Sheet 1 "DMUs." This new spreadsheet will contain data/funds. Once the fund names and data are pasted into the Excel spreadsheet, add a new worksheet called "Benchmarks," adjacent to the DMUs tab. Of the funds under examination in the DMUs sheet, two or three can be selected as benchmarks. These benchmarks can then be removed from the DMUs spreadsheet if required, and pasted into the Benchmarks spreadsheet, which will not affect the result. The scores will be generated in a new spreadsheet under a new tab called "Efficiency Report."

When using the RTS Region model, the results will be displayed under a new tab called "RTS Region." The selection of benchmarked funds is at the discretion of the investor, and can include a variety of fixed or variable models. Complete examples of each model are included in the CD-ROM, and new data can simply be pasted over the data provided in the examples.

If the fixed and variable benchmark models are selected you must create a new spreadsheet and rename Sheet 1 to DMUs which will contain your data/funds. Once the fund names and data are pasted in the excel spreadsheet a new worksheet called Benchmarks must be added adjacent to the DMUs tab. Of the funds under examination in the DMUs sheet two or three funds can be selected as benchmarks. The selected benchmarks can be removed from the DMUs spreadsheet, if required, and pasted into the Benchmarks spreadsheet, this will not affect the result. The scores will be generated in a new spreadsheet under a new tab called Efficiency Report. When using the RTS Region model the results are displayed under a new tab called RTS Region. The selection of benchmarked funds is at the discretion of the investor. The number of benchmarks can vary in either fixed or variable models. Complete examples of each model are included in the CD-ROM and new data can simply be pasted over the data provide in the examples.

CHAPTER 6

Application of Basic DEA Models

INTRODUCTION

Before addressing the variable returns-to-scale model, we summarize the constant returns-to-scale (CRS) model. A hedge fund or CTA is technically efficient if it maximizes output per unit of input. An output-oriented CRS shows by how much it is necessary to increase the output of the fund while keeping the inputs stable in order for an inefficient fund to become efficient. The best practices frontier contains the same efficient funds when using either an input- or output-oriented CRS model. CRS can be used if an investor or FOF manager believes that doubling the inputs will result in a proportionate doubling of outputs. Using either an input or output orientation will produce similar scores. A fund can be rendered efficient by diminishing the proportions of its inputs while maintaining constant the proportion of its outputs.

The VRS model in Chapter 2 ensures that the hedge fund or CTA is of similar scale as the fund being evaluated. If an increase in a fund's inputs does not result in a proportional adjustment in outputs, the fund displays variable returns-to-scale. This implies that as the hedge fund or CTA alters its level of operations, an increase or decrease in its efficiency could result.

The efficiency score obtained from the VRS model produces an efficiency score that is at least equivalent to that attained from the CRS model. The VRS efficiency scores are purely for technical efficiency (or managerial efficiency), which implies that the difference between the CRS and VRS overall scores is recognized to scale efficiency.

The reference set of an inefficient hedge fund or CTA is the set of efficient funds to which the inefficient hedge fund or CTA has been compared when calculating its efficiency score. It contains the efficient hedge funds and CTAs with the most similar input/output orientation to the inefficient fund, and should provide good examples of operating practice for the inefficient hedge fund and CTA to follow.

In the VRS model, the inefficient funds can produce different results under the input or output orientation. The measure of a fund's technical efficiency is calculated from the deviations of output from the best practices frontier. If a fund lies on the frontier, it is perfectly efficient; if it is below the frontier, it is technically inefficient.

Investors may prefer to use input-oriented models to indicate that an inefficient hedge fund or CTA can be made efficient by decreasing the magnitude of inputs while maintaining output magnitude constant. However, output-oriented models dictate that inefficient hedge funds or CTAs can be rendered efficient by increasing the magnitude of their outputs while keeping their input magnitude constant.

When selecting hedge funds, FOFs, or CTAs, investors must ascertain whether the fund managers have more control of their input decisions than their output decisions. In some cases, we may assume that a hedge fund manager or CTA can better control inputs than outputs given that we may prefer less risk during times of market turbulence. In the presence of bull markets, however, managers may desire to control outputs like compound return, and may prefer greater returns. Comparing CRS and VRS scores can certainly provide additional information about any hedge fund or CTA sources of inefficiency that a fund possesses.

RESULTS

Table 6.1 shows the input-oriented CRS and VRS efficient and non-efficient funds of hedge funds (FOFs). A score of 1.0 (100%) implies that funds are efficient; scores of less than 1.0 imply they are inefficient.

For example, in Table 6.1, Ironwood Partners, DKR International Relative Value (A), and Permal Japan Holdings are all efficient using the input-oriented CRS model. They represent the best practices frontier, and no other FOF generates the same output level for fewer inputs. Funds with the lowest scores are assumed to possess the greatest amount of inefficiency. For example, Coast Diversified Fund achieves an efficiency score of 93.68%, which means that the fund is 93.68% efficient using its inputs and outputs. This suggests the fund would have to diminish its inputs by 7.32% to be considered efficient.

Many funds that attain an efficiency score near 1.0 (or 100%) probably need only make minor corrections to their inputs to be considered efficient. But funds with scores well below 80% (for example, the GAM Diversity Fund, with an efficiency score of 51.077%) are notably far from efficient (and far from the best practices frontier). It may be feasible for these funds to perform input modifications and attain efficiency. But even funds with low scores may be able to attain efficiency if inputs are reduced while outputs (or return) are improved. DEA, essentially, gives a realistic representation of each fund's *degree* of inefficiency, which is a valuable tool for funds that hope to attain 1.0 (100%) efficiency.

Table 6.1 also includes the benchmarks to which each FOF is compared in both the CRS and VRS models. The benchmarked funds symbolize the fund or groups of funds to which the FOF should compare itself in order to become efficient. For example, the J. P. Morgan Multi-Strategy Fund can become efficient if it tries to emulate its two benchmarked funds (Ironwood Partners and DKR International Relative Value (A)). The J. P. Morgan Multi-Strategy Fund is strongly efficient when compared to its benchmarks, while the GAM Diversity Fund is weakly efficient when compared to its benchmark (DKR International Relative Value (A)). Efficient funds with a score of 1.0 are compared to themselves and are displayed in the benchmark column.

Examining the difference in scores between the models in Table 6.1 reveals that the VRS efficiency scores are higher than the CRS scores, as we expected. For example, the Asian Capital Holdings Fund is considered efficient if we assume VRS, but not if we assume CRS. Because the CRS model is more limiting than the VRS model, a greater number of funds will be rated efficient. This implies that funds may linearly scale their inputs and outputs without increasing or decreasing efficiency. Investors who wish to be more stringent in their manager selection process may compare the results of both models in terms of efficiency.

Table 6.2 presents the output-oriented CRS and VRS models. Funds with the smallest scores are considered efficient, while funds with scores greater than 1.0 are deemed inefficient. Three FOFs are rated efficient by using the CRS model (Ironwood Partners, DKR International Relative Value (A), and Permal Japan Holdings). These same funds are also efficient by using the VRS model, and three other FOFs are as well (Mesirow Event Strategies Fund, Edison Fund Class A, and Asian Capital Holdings).

The output-oriented VRS model produces six funds with an efficiency score of 1.0. For comparison purposes, we include the compounded return (in percent), dollars under management (ending), and the annualized Sharpe ratio in Table 6.2 for each of the remaining hedge fund and CTA classifications in this chapter (Tables 6.3 to 6.30). The same analysis can be applied to the remaining classifications in this chapter.

Table 6.31 compares the rankings and sensitivity of scores from both the CRS (input and output) and VRS (input and output) models using the Spearman rank correlation coefficient. We report one-tail *p*-values because we are confident that the correlations are positive. We find that a majority of hedge fund and CTA classifications have strong correlations. However, the market-neutral, global emerging, short-sellers, and agricultural are not significant. This is largely due to the high kurtosis (extraordinary gains and losses) of the market-neutral and global emerging categories, and the handful of funds in the short-sellers and agricultural classifications. Our robust results validate the precision of the various models used.

TABLE 6.1 Fund of Hedge Funds Input-Oriented CRS and VRS Models

DMU Name	Input-Oriented CRS Efficiency	Benchmark	Input-Oriented VRS Efficiency	Benchmark
GAM Diversity Fund	0.51077	DKR Intl Relative Value (A)	0.58156	Ironwood Partners, Edison Fund Class A, DKR Intl Relative Value (A)
Permal Investment Holdings NV (A)	0.58022	DKR Intl Relative Value (A)	0.71483	Asian Capital Holdings Fund, Edison Fund Class A
Haussman Holdings NV	0.62552	DKR Intl Relative Value (A)	0.74564	Edison Fund Class A, DKR Intl Relative Value (A)
Mesirow Alternative Strategies Fund	0.74107	DKR Intl Relative Value (A)	0.74107	DKR Intl Relative Value (A)
JP Morgan Multi-Strategy Fund	0.82093	Ironwood Partners, DKR Intl Relative Value (A)	0.87291	Ironwood Partners, DKR Intl Relative Value (A), Edison Fund Class A
Man-Glenwood Multi-Strategy Fund	0.56552	DKR Intl Relative Value (A)	0.57104	Edison Fund Class A, DKR Intl Relative Value (A)
Coast Diversified Fund	0.93682	Ironwood Partners	0.97038	Ironwood Partners, DKR Intl Relative Value (A), Edison Fund Class A
Aurora	0.69691	DKR Intl Relative Value (A)	0.74769	Ironwood Partners, DKR Intl Relative Value (A), Edison Fund Class A
Lighthouse Diversified Fund	0.76368	DKR Intl Relative Value (A)	0.78678	Ironwood Partners, DKR Intl Relative Value (A), Edison Fund Class A

Fund				
Mesirow Equity Opportunity Fund	0.75846	DKR Intl Relative Value (A)	0.82854	Ironwood Partners, DKR Intl Relative Value (A), Edison Fund Class A
Meridian Horizon Fund	0.69107	DKR Intl Relative Value (A)	0.90619	Ironwood Partners, Edison Fund Class A, Asian Capital Holdings Fund
Leveraged Capital Holdings	0.61096	DKR Intl Relative Value (A)	0.76642	Asian Capital Holdings Fund, Edison Fund Class A
Ironwood Partners	1.00000	Ironwood Partners	1.00000	Ironwood Partners
DKR Intl Relative Value (A)	1.00000	DKR Intl Relative Value (A)	0.90265	DKR Intl Relative Value (A)
Mesirow Event Strategies Fund	0.79175	DKR Intl Relative Value (A)	0.93687	Ironwood Partners
Momentum All Weather Fund	0.92701	DKR Intl Relative Value (A)	1.00000	Ironwood Partners, DKR Intl Relative Value (A)
Edison Fund Class A	0.84130	DKR Intl Relative Value (A)	0.61051	Edison Fund Class A
Green Way Class B (Euro)	0.60274	DKR Intl Relative Value (A)	1.00000	Edison Fund Class A, DKR Intl Relative Value (A)
Permal Japan Holdings	1.00000	Permal Japan Holdings	1.00000	Permal Japan Holdings
Asian Capital Holdings Fund	0.80281	Permal Japan Holdings, DKR Intl Relative Value (A)		Asian Capital Holdings Fund

TABLE 6.2 Fund of Hedge Funds Output-Oriented CRS and VRS Models

DMU Name	Output-Oriented CRS Efficiency	Output-Oriented VRS Efficiency	Compounded Return	Dollars Under Management	Annualized Sharpe Ratio
GAM Diversity Fund	1.95783	1.12511	91.61	$2,963,150,000	0.64
Permal Investment Holdings NV (A)	1.72349	1.15818	62.65	$2,900,000,000	0.27
Haussman Holdings NV	1.59867	1.24055	48.71	$2,700,000,000	0.17
Mesirow Alternative Strategies Fund	1.34940	1.05972	61.46	$2,207,000,000	0.66
JP Morgan Multi-Strategy Fund	1.21813	1.10355	87.20	$2,184,610,000	1.14
Man-Glenwood Multi-Strategy Fund	1.76827	1.21350	43.35	$2,132,103,000	0.15
Coast Diversified Fund	1.06744	1.02144	91.60	$1,579,610,000	1.42
Aurora	1.43490	1.08053	87.21	$1,404,000,000	1.00
Lighthouse Diversified Fund	1.30945	1.07239	83.94	$1,260,000,000	1.15
Mesirow Equity Opportunity Fund	1.31847	1.12819	88.49	$1,168,900,000	1.03
Meridian Horizon Fund	1.44703	1.02947	121.27	$1,145,600,000	1.22
Leveraged Capital Holdings	1.63678	1.19495	48.23	$1,079,000,000	0.16
Ironwood Partners	1.00000	1.00000	104.45	$992,000,000	1.76
DKR Intl Relative Value (A)	1.00000	1.00000	90.76	$956,200,000	1.77
Mesirow Event Strategies Fund	1.26303	1.00000	94.06	$918,100,000	1.39
Momentum All Weather Fund	1.07873	1.02295	54.27	$889,783,000	0.54
Green Way Class B {Euro}	1.65908	1.27454	43.17	$817,000,000	0.15
Edison Fund Class A	1.18863	1.00000	296.35	$763,980,000	2.03
Permal Japan Holdings	1.00000	1.00000	97.54	$753,000,000	0.49
Asian Capital Holdings Fund	1.24563	1.00000	69.73	$722,235,000	0.29

TABLE 6.3 Event-Driven Input-Oriented CRS and VRS Models

DMU Name	Input-Oriented CRS Efficiency	Benchmark	Input-Oriented VRS Efficiency	Benchmark
King Street Capital Ltd	1.00000	King Street Capital Ltd	1.00000	King Street Capital Ltd
Elliott Intl	0.64042	King Street Capital, Caspian Capital Partners	0.69216	King Street Capital Ltd, Caspian Capital Partners
Canyon Value Realization Cayman (A)	0.42892	Caspian Capital Partners	0.50678	York Select, Caspian Capital Partners
Elliott Associates	0.64292	King Street Capital, Caspian Capital Partners	0.69537	King Street Capital Ltd, Caspian Capital Partners
York Investment	0.73069	King Street Capital, Caspian Capital Partners	0.88345	King Street Capital, York Select, Caspian Capital Partners
King Street Capital	1.00000	King Street Capital	1.00000	King Street Capital
Paulson Intl	0.57098	Caspian Capital Partners	0.69080	York Select, Caspian Capital Partners
Canyon Value Realization Cayman (B)	0.42892	Caspian Capital Partners	0.50678	York Select, Caspian Capital Partners
Canyon Value Realization Fund	0.46373	Caspian Capital Partners	0.56607	York Select, Caspian Capital Partners
Halcyon Offshore Event-Driven Strat	0.63949	King Street Capital, Caspian Capital Partners	0.65788	King Street Capital Ltd, Caspian Capital Partners

TABLE 6.3 (Continued)

DMU Name	Input-Oriented CRS Efficiency	Benchmark	Input-Oriented VRS Efficiency	Benchmark
York Select	0.72257	King Street Capital, Caspian Capital Partners	1.00000	York Select
York Capital Mgt	0.72667	King Street Capital, Caspian Capital Partners	0.87757	King Street Capital, York Select, Caspian Capital Partners
Caspian Capital Partners	1.00000	Caspian Capital Partners	1.00000	Caspian Capital Partners
Paulson Partners	0.55924	Caspian Capital Partners	0.67350	York Select, Caspian Capital Partners
Halcyon Fund	0.73214	King Street Capital, Caspian Capital Partners	0.77693	King Street Capital, York Select, Caspian Capital Partners
GAM Arbitrage	0.51648	Caspian Capital Partners	0.51648	Caspian Capital Partners
Triage Capital Mgt	0.77765	King Street Capital, Caspian Capital Partners	0.98671	King Street Capital, York Select, Caspian Capital Partners
Gabelli Associates	0.73989	Caspian Capital Partners	0.83929	Caspian Capital Partners
Corsair Capital Partners (CCA)	0.65649	King Street Capital, Caspian Capital Partners	0.97077	York Select, Caspian Capital Partners
American Durham	0.61566	King Street Capital, Caspian Capital Partners	0.65172	King Street Capital Ltd, Caspian Capital Partners

TABLE 6.4 Event-Driven Output-Oriented CRS and VRS Models

DMU Name	Output-Oriented CRS Efficiency	Output-Oriented VRS Efficiency	Compounded Return	Dollars Under Management	Annualized Sharpe Ratio
King Street Capital Ltd	1.00000	1.00000	107.32	$3,128,000,000	1.64
Elliott Intl	1.56149	1.11338	90.98	$2,415,000,000	1.08
Canyon Value Realization Cayman (A)	2.33146	1.15893	75.80	$1,757,000,000	0.47
Elliott Associates	1.55541	1.11338	90.70	$1,695,000,000	1.08
York Investment	1.36857	1.09988	104.41	$1,520,000,000	0.82
King Street Capital	1.00000	1.00000	126.23	$1,425,000,000	1.87
Paulson Intl	1.75136	1.16629	99.10	$1,369,000,000	0.85
Canyon Value Realization Cayman (B)	2.33146	1.17419	71.43	$1,119,000,000	0.43
Canyon Value Realization Fund	2.15643	1.16317	82.02	$1,012,000,000	0.54
Halcyon Offshore Event-Driven Strat	1.56375	1.19131	82.19	$671,600,000	0.90
York Select	1.38394	1.00000	237.98	$480,000,000	0.99
York Capital Mgt	1.37614	1.10545	112.25	$400,000,000	0.88
Caspian Capital Partners	1.00000	1.00000	165.12	$397,000,000	3.15
Paulson Partners	1.78815	1.16786	96.40	$359,500,000	0.81
Halcyon Fund	1.36585	1.19080	90.26	$284,200,000	0.91
GAM Arbitrage	1.93617	1.13974	91.09	$283,380,000	0.84
Triage Capital Mgt	1.28592	1.01068	164.21	$261,000,000	1.14
Gabelli Associates	1.35156	1.13434	74.79	$238,350,000	0.98
Corsair Capital Partners (CCA)	1.52324	1.02316	163.05	$233,000,000	0.88
American Durham	1.62427	1.26731	58.69	$205,000,000	0.45

TABLE 6.5 Market-Neutral Input-Oriented CRS and VRS Models

DMU Name	Input-Oriented CRS Efficiency	Benchmark	Input-Oriented VRS Efficiency	Benchmark
Derivative Arbitrage Fund {Yen}	0.69174	MBS Fund Gamma (O), Black Diamond	0.71600	Millennium Intl, Alta Partners Ltd, Black Diamond
Ellington Composite	0.32231	Millennium Intl, MBS Fund Gamma (O)	1.00000	Ellington Composite
Millennium Intl	1.00000	Millennium Intl	1.00000	Millennium Intl
Shepherd Investments Intl	0.72700	Millennium Intl, MBS Fund Gamma (O)	0.73109	Millennium Intl, MBS Fund Gamma (O)
Deephaven Market Neutral Fund Ltd	0.83959	Millennium Intl, MBS Fund Gamma (O)	0.83959	Millennium Intl, MBS Fund Gamma (O)
Alexandra Global Master Fund	1.00000	Alexandra Global Master Fund	1.00000	Alexandra Global Master Fund
Stark Investments	0.72022	Millennium Intl, MBS Fund Gamma (O)	0.72489	Millennium Intl, MBS Fund Gamma (O)
III Fund Ltd	0.56234	Millennium Intl, MBS Fund Gamma (O)	0.56787	Millennium Intl, MBS Fund Gamma (O)
III Global	0.47373	Millennium Intl, MBS Fund Gamma (O)	0.47879	Millennium Intl, MBS Fund Gamma (O)

Ellington Overseas Partners

Ellington Overseas Partners	1.00000	
MBS Fund Gamma (O)	1.00000	MBS Fund Gamma (O)
Alta Partners Ltd	1.00000	Alta Partners Ltd
Libertyview Plus Fund	0.73660	Millennium Intl, MBS Fund Gamma (O)
Deephaven Market Neutral Fund	0.82257	Millennium Intl, MBS Fund Gamma (O)
Double Black Diamond	0.89597	Millennium Intl, MBS Fund Gamma (O), Black Diamond
St Albans Partners	0.94477	Millennium Intl, MBS Fund Gamma (O), Black Diamond
Mkt Neutral Equitized Strat Comp	1.00000	Mkt Neutral Equitized Strat Comp
Concordia Capital (A)	1.00000	Concordia Capital (A)
Argent Classic Conv ARB(Bermuda) (A)	1.00000	Argent Classic Conv ARB(Bermuda) (A)
Black Diamond	1.00000	Black Diamond

Ellington Overseas Partners	0.32741	Millennium Intl, MBS Fund Gamma (O)
MBS Fund Gamma (O)	1.00000	MBS Fund Gamma (O)
Alta Partners Ltd	1.00000	Alta Partners Ltd
Libertyview Plus Fund	0.73285	Millennium Intl, MBS Fund Gamma (O)
Deephaven Market Neutral Fund	0.82257	Millennium Intl, MBS Fund Gamma (O)
Double Black Diamond	0.89226	Millennium Intl, MBS Fund Gamma (O), Black Diamond
St Albans Partners	0.94150	MBS Fund Gamma (O), Black Diamond
Mkt Neutral Equitized Strat Comp	0.65562	MBS Fund Gamma (O), Black Diamond
Concordia Capital (A)	0.73784	Millennium Intl, MBS Fund Gamma (O)
Argent Classic Conv Arb(Bermuda) (A)	0.69417	MBS Fund Gamma (O), Black Diamond
Black Diamond	1.00000	Black Diamond

TABLE 6.6 Market-Neutral Output-Oriented CRS and VRS Models

DMU Name	Output-Oriented CRS Efficiency	Output-Oriented VRS Efficiency	Compounded Return	Dollars Under Management	Annualized Sharpe Ratio
Derivative Arbitrage Fund (Yen)	1.44563	1.23152	53.72	$3,697,439,000	0.26
Ellington Composite	3.10260	1.00000	67.72	$2,704,140,000	0.36
Millennium Intl	1.00000	1.00000	213.75	$2,598,068,000	2.35
Shepherd Investments Intl	1.37552	1.09943	108.26	$2,593,440,000	1.00
Deephaven Market Neutral Fund Ltd	1.19106	1.01244	131.55	$1,858,676,000	1.50
Alexandra Global Master Fund	1.00000	1.00000	128.07	$1,705,000,000	1.51
Stark Investments	1.38847	1.09090	112.04	$1,515,830,000	0.95
III Fund Ltd	1.77828	1.03811	74.35	$1,461,737,000	0.56
III Global	2.11089	1.03651	79.63	$996,251,000	0.45
Ellington Overseas Partners	3.05427	1.00000	40.91	$971,000,000	0.11
MBS Fund Gamma (O)	1.00000	1.00000	33.43	$967,585,000	−0.31
Alta Partners Ltd	1.00000	1.00000	219.62	$959,574,000	1.80
Libertyview Plus Fund	1.36453	1.08187	50.93	$928,036,000	0.47
Deephaven Market Neutral Fund	1.21570	1.01193	133.87	$873,718,000	1.46
Double Black Diamond	1.12075	1.07136	108.88	$736,400,000	1.47
St Albans Partners	1.06213	1.05810	68.38	$695,000,000	0.95
Mkt Neutral Equitized Strat Comp	1.52528	1.00000	22.14	$644,277,000	−0.02
Concordia Capital (A)	1.35530	1.00000	69.12	$548,000,000	0.95
Argent Classic Conv ARB(Bermuda) (A)	1.44057	1.00000	164.97	$519,106,000	0.94
Black Diamond	1.00000	1.00000	61.66	$466,000,000	0.99

TABLE 6.7 Global Macro Input-Oriented CRS and VRS Models

DMU Name	Input-Oriented CRS Efficiency	Benchmark	Input-Oriented VRS Efficiency	Benchmark
Vega Global Fund	1.00000	Vega Global Fund	1.00000	Vega Global Fund
UBS Currency Portfolio	0.77177	Gamut Investments	0.82321	Vega Global Fund, Gamut Investments
Gamut Investments	1.00000	Gamut Investments	1.00000	Gamut Investments
Global Undervalued Securities Fund	1.00000	Global Undervalued Securities Fund	1.00000	Global Undervalued Securities Fund
LCM GL INT Rate Hedged Fund (Opport)	0.86197	Vega Global Fund, Gamut Investments, Global Undervalued Securities Fund	0.88696	Vega Global Fund, Gamut Investments, Global Undervalued Securities Fund
CRG Partners LDC	0.78728	Gamut Investments	0.86805	Gamut Investments, Quadriga Ag {Euro}, Peak Partners
Permal Europe {Euro}	0.72490	Gamut Investments	0.75065	Gamut Investments, Global Undervalued Securities Fund, Quadriga AG {Euro}
Wexford Offshore Spectrum Fund	0.76238	Gamut Investments	0.78148	Vega Global Fund, Gamut Investments
Wexford Spectrum Fund	0.76090	Gamut Investments	0.77157	Vega Global Fund, Gamut Investments
Quadriga AG {Euro}	0.85855	Gamut Investments	1.00000	Quadriga AG {Euro}
Peak Partners	0.82069	Gamut Investments	1.00000	Peak Partners
GAM Cross-Market	0.79949	Vega Global Fund, Gamut Investments, Global Undervalued Securities Fund	0.82886	Vega Global Fund, Gamut Global Investments, Undervalued Securities Fund
Grossman Currency Fund	0.78035	Gamut Investments	0.84171	Gamut Investments, Quadriga AG {Euro}
Universal Bond Fund	0.60322	Gamut Investments	0.61502	Gamut Investments, Quadriga AG {Euro}

TABLE 6.8 Global Macro Output-Oriented CRS and VRS Models

DMU Name	Output-Oriented CRS Efficiency	Output-Oriented VRS Efficiency	Compounded Return	Dollars Under Management	Annualized Sharpe Ratio
Vega Global Fund	1.00000	1.00000	70.19	$4,159,280,000	0.75
UBS Currency Portfolio	1.29572	1.24468	46.43	$1,829,000,000	0.16
Gamut Investments	1.00000	1.00000	224.65	$1,028,800,000	1.75
Global Undervalued Securities Fund	1.00000	1.15615	515.17	$944,900,000	0.84
LCM Gl Int Rate Hedged Fund (Opport)	1.16013	1.08891	70.38	$852,880,000	0.44
CRG Partners Ldc	1.27019	1.19846	141.00	$713,109,000	0.70
Permal Europe {Euro}	1.37951	1.15365	88.53	$474,462,000	0.46
Wexford Offshore Spectrum Fund	1.31168	1.15040	128.52	$296,500,000	0.88
Wexford Spectrum Fund	1.31423	1.00000	135.53	$268,300,000	0.90
Quadriga AG {Euro}	1.16476	1.00000	392.95	$179,400,000	0.89
Peak Partners	1.21849	1.14849	220.43	$175,250,000	0.85
GAM Cross-Market	1.25080	1.13925	94.99	$125,000,000	0.62
Grossman Currency Fund	1.28148	1.29492	110.07	$109,000,000	0.52
Universal Bond Fund	1.65776		31.35	$34,202,000	0.02

TABLE 6.9 Global Emerging Input-Oriented CRS and VRS Models

DMU Name	Input-Oriented CRS Efficiency	Benchmark	Input-Oriented VRS Efficiency	Benchmark
Ashmore Emerg. Markets Liquid Invest	0.78152	LIM Asia Arbitrage Fund, Futurewatch	0.78780	LIM Asia Arbitrage Fund, Futurewatch
Hermitage Fund (Worst Bid)	0.72614	Futurewatch	0.88295	Tradewinds Russia Partners I, Futurewatch
Ashmore Local Currency Debt Port	0.66987	LIM Asia Arbitrage Fund, Futurewatch	1.00000	Ashmore Local Currency Debt Port
LIM Asia Arbitrage Fund	1.00000	LIM Asia Arbitrage Fund	1.00000	LIM Asia Arbitrage Fund
GLS Offshore Global Opportunities	0.74403	LIM Asia Arbitrage Fund, Futurewatch	0.75491	LIM Asia Arbitrage Fund, Futurewatch
Consulta Emerging Markets Debt	0.72117	LIM Asia Arbitrage Fund, Futurewatch	0.74865	LIM Asia Arbitrage Fund, Greylock Global Opportunity Fund, Futurewatch
Firebird Republics Fund	0.65659	LIM Asia Arbitrage Fund, Futurewatch	0.65881	LIM Asia Arbitrage Fund, Futurewatch
Firebird New Russia Fund	0.67222	Futurewatch	0.86705	Greylock Global Opportunity Fund, Ashmore Russian Debt Portfolio, Tradewinds Russia Partners I, Futurewatch
Greylock Global Opportunity Fund	0.76186	LIM Asia Arbitrage Fund, Futurewatch	1.00000	Greylock Global Opportunity Fund
EK Asia Fund	0.92617	LIM Asia Arbitrage Fund, Futurewatch	0.94201	LIM Asia Arbitrage Fund, Futurewatch

TABLE 6.9 (*Continued*)

DMU Name	Input-Oriented CRS Efficiency	Benchmark	Input-Oriented VRS Efficiency	Benchmark
GLS Global Opportunities Fund	0.68876	LIM Asia Arbitrage Fund, Futurewatch	0.69850	LIM Asia Arbitrage Fund, Futurewatch
Griffin East European Value (Euro)	0.74541	Futurewatch	0.76601	Tradewinds Russia Partners I, Futurewatch
Tiedemann/Ayer Asian Growth	0.75873	LIM Asia Arbitrage Fund, Futurewatch	0.77591	LIM Asia Arbitrage Fund, Futurewatch
Key Global Emerging Markets	0.67152	LIM Asia Arbitrage Fund, Futurewatch	0.68815	LIM Asia Arbitrage Fund, Futurewatch
Firebird Fund	0.74243	Futurewatch	0.89893	Tradewinds Russia Partners I, Futurewatch
Ashmore Russian Debt Portfolio	0.57721	LIM Asia Arbitrage Fund, Futurewatch	1.00000	Ashmore Russian Debt Portfolio
Tradewinds Russia Partners I	0.74918	Futurewatch	1.00000	Tradewinds Russia Partners I
Futurewatch	1.00000	Futurewatch	1.00000	Futurewatch
Post Communist Opportunities Fund	0.80647	LIM Asia Arbitrage Fund, Futurewatch	0.81331	LIM Asia Arbitrage Fund, Futurewatch
Opportunity Fund Brazilian Hedge	1.00000	Opportunity Fund Brazilian Hedge	1.00000	Opportunity Fund Brazilian Hedge

TABLE 6.10 Global Emerging Output-Oriented CRS and VRS Models

DMU Name	Output-Oriented CRS Efficiency	Output-Oriented VRS Efficiency	Compounded Return	Dollars Under Management	Annualized Sharpe Ratio
Ashmore Emerg Markets Liquid Invest	1.27955	1.11380	162.27	$1,722,000,000	0.66
Hermitage Fund (Worst Bid)	1.37715	1.03457	36.66	$1,133,062,000	0.31
Ashmore Local Currency Debt Port	1.49283	1.00000	128.84	$309,000,000	0.57
LIM Asia Arbitrage Fund	1.00000	1.00000	98.32	$297,300,000	0.95
GLS Offshore Global Opportunities	1.34403	1.21863	68.31	$223,792,000	0.26
Consulta Emerging Markets Debt	1.38663	1.04323	207.28	$220,000,000	0.82
Firebird Republics Fund	1.52301	1.10885	94.56	$191,600,000	0.34
Firebird New Russia Fund	1.48760	1.02755	193.94	$147,400,000	0.50
Greylock Global Opportunity Fund	1.31259	1.00000	203.23	$121,000,000	0.93
EK Asia Fund	1.07971	1.06959	123.77	$111,000,000	0.61
GLS Global Opportunities Fund	1.45187	1.22849	47.49	$95,098,000	0.19
Griffin East European Value (Euro)	1.34154	1.05679	143.69	$94,850,000	0.44
Tiedemann/Ayer Asian Growth	1.31799	1.29269	42.80	$92,458,000	0.12
Key Global Emerging Markets	1.48915	1.30286	38.64	$86,553,000	0.10
Firebird Fund	1.34694	1.04435	135.97	$58,600,000	0.43
Ashmore Russian Debt Portfolio	1.73248	1.00000	301.53	$57,000,000	0.63
Tradewinds Russia Partners I	1.33479	1.00000	25.77	$54,000,000	0.38
Futurewatch	1.00000	1.00000	832.48	$51,914,000	1.32
Post Communist Opportunities Fund	1.23998	1.15252	111.36	$43,510,000	0.38
Opportunity Fund Brazilian Hedge	1.00000	1.00000	103.95	$30,552,000	0.50

TABLE 6.11 Global Established Input-Oriented CRS and VRS Models

DMU Name	Input-Oriented CRS Efficiency	Benchmark	Input-Oriented VRS Efficiency	Benchmark
Eureka Fund {Euro}	1.00000	Eureka Fund {Euro}	1.00000	Eureka Fund {Euro}
Eureka Fund	1.00000	Eureka Fund	1.00000	Eureka Fund
Cobalt Partners	1.00000	Cobalt Partners	1.00000	Cobalt Partners
Steel Partners II	0.93270	Eureka Fund, Amici Associates, Seminole Capital Partners	0.99822	Eureka Fund, Libra Fund, Seminole Capital Partners, New Star Hedge Fund {BP}
Adelphi Europe Fund (B) {Euro}	0.86731	Eureka Fund, Amici Associates, Seminole Capital Partners	0.88826	Eureka Fund {Euro}, Seminole Capital Partners
Cobalt Offshore Fund	0.97230	Eureka Fund, Cobalt Partners, Seminole Capital Partners	0.97935	Cobalt Partners, Odey European {Euro}
Odey European {Euro}	0.91614	Eureka Fund {Euro}, Cobalt Partners	1.00000	Odey European {Euro}
First Eagle Fund NV	0.81814	Amici Associates, Seminole Capital Partners	0.86205	Eureka Fund, Libra Fund, Seminole Capital Partners, New Star Hedge Fund {BP}
Pegasus Fund {BP}	0.84938	Eureka Fund {Euro}, Seminole Capital Partners	1.00000	Pegasus Fund {BP}
Libra Fund	0.86469	Eureka Fund, Amici Associates, Seminole Capital Partners	1.00000	Libra Fund
Eagle Capital Partners	0.91295	Eureka Fund, Amici Associates, Seminole Capital Partners	0.94970	Eureka Fund, Libra Fund, New Star Hedge Fund {BP}

AJR International (A)	0.82378	Eureka Fund, Amici Associates	0.95296	Libra Fund, Cambrian Fund (A), Seminole Capital Partners
Amici Associates	1.00000	Amici Associates	1.00000	Amici Associates
Cambrian Fund (A)	0.77857	Amici Associates, Seminole Capital Partners	1.00000	Cambrian Fund (A)
Seminole Capital Partners	1.00000	Seminole Capital Partners	1.00000	Seminole Capital Partners
Everglades Partners	0.86742	Eureka Fund, Amici Associates, Seminole Capital Partners	0.86818	Eureka Fund, Amici Associates, Seminole Capital Partners
Giano Capital {Euro}	0.90391	Eureka Fund, Amici Associates, Seminole Capital Partners	0.90688	Amici Associates, Seminole Capital Partners, New Star Hedge Fund {BP}
Adelphi Europe Fund (A)	0.89342	Eureka Fund, Amici Associates, Seminole Capital Partners	0.89434	Eureka Fund, Amici Associates, Seminole Capital Partners
Bricoleur Offshore	0.83661	Eureka Fund, Amici Associates,	0.85510	Eureka Fund, Cobalt Partners, Amici Associates
New Star Hedge Fund {BP}	0.98055	Eureka Fund, Amici Associates,	1.00000	New Star Hedge Fund {BP}

TABLE 6.12 Global Established Output-Oriented CRS and VRS Models

DMU Name	Output-Oriented CRS Efficiency	Output-Oriented VRS Efficiency	Compounded Return	Dollars Under Management	Annualized Sharpe Ratio
Eureka Fund {Euro}	1.00000	1.00000	219.33	$2,478,000,000	1.34
Eureka Fund	1.00000	1.00000	237.65	$1,031,000,000	1.42
Cobalt Partners	1.00000	1.00000	173.36	$668,300,000	1.13
Steel Partners II	1.07216	1.00093	192.16	$544,200,000	0.89
Adelphi Europe Fund (B) {Euro}	1.15299	1.12492	122.53	$539,300,000	0.61
Cobalt Offshore Fund	1.02848	1.01642	160.56	$510,377,000	1.04
Odey European {Euro}	1.09154	1.00000	103.28	$506,660,000	0.67
First Eagle Fund NV	1.22229	1.08607	79.55	$494,800,000	0.32
Pegasus Fund {BP}	1.17732	1.00000	165.77	$450,000,000	0.59
Libra Fund	1.15649	1.00000	333.52	$441,110,000	0.96
Eagle Capital Partners	1.09535	1.02536	162.13	$392,000,000	0.82
AJR International (A)	1.21392	1.02120	185.46	$388,900,000	0.66
Amici Associates	1.00000	1.00000	137.79	$388,000,000	0.84
Cambrian Fund (A)	1.28440	1.00000	218.11	$358,900,000	0.64
Seminole Capital Partners	1.00000	1.00000	219.03	$350,000,000	0.89
Everglades Partners	1.15285	1.04417	125.33	$308,000,000	0.70
Giano Capital {Euro}	1.10630	1.08377	119.79	$283,168,000	0.59
Adelphi Europe Fund (A)	1.11929	1.11133	114.73	$276,800,000	0.57
Bricoleur Offshore	1.19530	1.11718	91.95	$272,000,000	0.49
New Star Hedge Fund {BP}	1.01984	1.00000	182.60	$245,351,000	0.86

TABLE 6.13 Global International Input-Oriented CRS and VRS Models

DMU Name	Input-Oriented CRS Efficiency	Benchmark	Input-Oriented VRS Efficiency	Benchmark
Orbis Global Equity	0.83532	Platinum Fund	0.95433	Platinum Fund, Equinox Partners, Performance Partners
Orbis Optimal (US)	0.91258	Platinum Fund, Performance Partners	0.97394	Orbis Leveraged (US), Platinum Fund, IIU Convertible Fund, Performance Partners
Orbis Leveraged (US)	0.87038	Platinum Fund, Performance Partners	1.00000	Orbis Leveraged (US)
Platinum Fund	1.00000	Platinum Fund	1.00000	Platinum Fund
Lazard Global Opportunities Ltd	0.80945	Platinum Fund, Performance Partners	0.81742	Platinum Fund, Stewart Asian Holdings, Performance Partners
Lazard Global Opportunities	0.83786	Platinum Fund, Performance Partners	0.84068	Platinum Fund, Stewart Asian Holdings, Performance Partners
IIU Convertible Fund	1.00000	IIU Convertible Fund	1.00000	IIU Convertible Fund
GAM Selection	0.79667	Platinum Fund, Performance Partners	0.80231	Platinum Fund, Performance Partners
Equinox Partners	0.83547	Platinum Fund	1.00000	Equinox Partners

TABLE 6.13 *(Continued)*

DMU Name	Input-Oriented CRS Efficiency	Benchmark	Input-Oriented VRS Efficiency	Benchmark
Glenrock Global Partners	0.71545	Platinum Fund, Performance Partners	0.73791	Platinum Fund, Equinox Partners, Stewart Asian Holdings
Glenrock Global Partners (BVI)	0.71277	Platinum Fund, Performance Partners	0.73389	Platinum Fund, Equinox Partners, Stewart Asian Holdings
Third Avenue Global Value Fund	0.89615	Platinum Fund, Performance Partners	0.93836	Platinum Fund, Stewart Asian Holdings, Polaris Prime Europe, Performance Partners
Stewart Asian Holdings	1.00000	Stewart Asian Holdings	1.00000	Stewart Asian Holdings
Millburn Intl Stock Index Fund	0.75419	Platinum Fund, Performance Partners	0.75567	Platinum Fund, Stewart Asian Holdings, Performance Partners
Polaris Prime Europe	1.00000	Polaris Prime Europe	1.00000	Polaris Prime Europe
Zazove Global Convertible Fund	0.82628	Platinum Fund, Performance Partners	0.83118	Platinum Fund, Performance Partners
Aravis Clipper Fund	0.64691	Platinum Fund, Performance Partners	0.74826	Platinum Fund, Equinox Partners, Polaris Prime Europe, Performance Partners
Performance Partners	1.00000	Performance Partners	1.00000	Performance Partners

TABLE 6.14 Global International Output-Oriented CRS and VRS Models

DMU Name	Output-Oriented CRS Efficiency	Output-Oriented VRS Efficiency	Compounded Return	Dollars Under Management	Annualized Sharpe Ratio
Orbis Global Equity	1.19715	1.00374	174.53	$3,909,700,000	0.67
Orbis Optimal {US}	1.09579	1.00148	148.24	$3,236,600,000	0.96
Orbis Leveraged {US}	1.14893	1.00000	301.33	$874,100,000	0.87
Platinum Fund	1.00000	1.00000	221.52	$716,800,000	1.10
Lazard Global Opportunities Ltd	1.23541	1.06784	141.94	$499,830,000	0.68
Lazard Global Opportunities	1.19352	1.06782	133.45	$376,077,000	0.66
IIU Convertible Fund	1.00000	1.00000	160.34	$142,000,000	0.99
GAM Selection	1.25522	1.14652	63.88	$84,070,000	0.26
Equinox Partners	1.19693	1.00000	274.45	$71,800,000	0.64
Glenrock Global Partners	1.39773	1.09257	55.48	$69,600,000	0.20
Glenrock Global Partners (BVI)	1.40298	1.09281	56.03	$53,500,000	0.20
Third Avenue Global Value Fund	1.11588	1.02500	175.31	$31,583,000	0.81
Stewart Asian Holdings	1.00000	1.00000	78.50	$18,522,000	0.28
Millburn Intl Stock Index Fund	1.32592	1.15001	27.83	$10,821,000	0.01
Polaris Prime Europe	1.00000	1.00000	600.43	$10,460,000	0.69
Zazove Global Convertible Fund	1.21024	1.12037	95.22	$9,000,000	0.47
Aravis Clipper Fund	1.54580	1.00716	63.03	$5,177,000	0.25
Performance Partners	1.00000	1.00000	120.26	$3,100,000	0.98

TABLE 6.15 Sector Input-Oriented CRS and VRS Models

DMU Name	Input-Oriented CRS Efficiency	Benchmark	Input-Oriented VRS Efficiency	Benchmark
Sandler Associates	1.00000	Sandler Associates	1.00000	Sandler Associates
Spinner Global Technology Fund	1.00000	Spinner Global Technology Fund	1.00000	Spinner Global Technology Fund
Basswood Financial Partners	0.86820	Sandler Associates, Malta Hedge Fund II	0.88674	Sandler Associates, Malta Hedge Fund II
Sandler Offshore	1.00000	Sandler Offshore	1.00000	Sandler Offshore
Caduceus Capital Ltd	0.95231	Sandler Associates, KCM Biomedical, Galleon Omni Technology Fund (A)	1.00000	Caduceus Capital Ltd
KCM Biomedical	1.00000	KCM Biomedical	1.00000	KCM Biomedical
Malta Hedge Fund II	1.00000	Malta Hedge Fund II	1.00000	Malta Hedge Fund Ii
FBR Ashton	0.86714	Sandler Associates, Spinner Global Technology Fund	0.95735	Spinner Global Technology Fund, Caduceus Capital, Dynamis Fund
Keefe-Rainbow Partners	0.73703	Sandler Associates, Malta Hedge Fund II	0.75572	Sandler Associates, Malta Hedge Fund II, Acadia Fund
Acadia Fund	1.00000	Acadia Fund	1.00000	Acadia Fund
Caduceus Capital	0.97267	Sandler Associates, KCM Biomedical, Galleon Omni Technology Fund (A)	1.00000	Caduceus Capital
Dynamis Fund	0.83462	Sandler Associates, Spinner Global Technology Fund	1.00000	Dynamis Fund

Financial Stocks	0.69360	Sandler Associates, Spinner Global Technology Fund	0.74803	Spinner Global Technology Fund, Acadia Fund, Dynamis Fund
Hangar 4 Eagle I	0.98146	Sandler Offshore, Galleon Omni Technology Fund (A)	1.00000	Hangar 4 Eagle I
Financial Edge Fund	0.70057	Sandler Offshore, Malta Hedge Fund II, Galleon Omni Technology Fund (A)	1.00000	Financial Edge Fund
Crestwood Capital Intl	0.95901	Sandler Associates, Spinner Global Technology Fund	0.95929	Sandler Associates, Spinner Global Technology Fund, Sandler Offshore
Digital Century Capital	0.79249	Sandler Associates	0.94209	Spinner Global Technology Fund, Dynamis Fund
Galleon Omni Technology Fund (A)	1.00000	Galleon Omni Technology Fund (A)	1.00000	Galleon Omni Technology Fund (A)
America First Fin Institutions Invest.	0.81974	Sandler Associates	0.83506	Sandler Associates, Spinner Global Technology Fund
Polaris Prime Technology	0.91300	Spinner Global Technology Fund, Sandler Offshore, Malta Hedge Fund II, Galleon Omni Technology Fund (A)	1.00000	Polaris Prime Technology

TABLE 6.16 Sector Output-Oriented CRS and VRS Models

DMU Name	Output-Oriented CRS Efficiency	Output-Oriented VRS Efficiency	Compounded Return	Dollars Under Management	Annualized Sharpe Ratio
Sandler Associates	1.00000	1.00000	186.63	$459,000,000	1.07
Spinner Global Technology Fund	1.00000	1.00000	215.17	$319,200,000	0.73
Basswood Financial Partners	1.15181	1.09871	86.93	$291,000,000	0.45
Sandler Offshore	1.00000	1.00000	182.02	$284,000,000	1.06
Caduceus Capital Ltd	1.05008	1.00000	340.57	$220,000,000	0.71
KCM Biomedical	1.00000	1.00000	301.95	$159,500,000	0.63
Malta Hedge Fund II	1.00000	1.00000	102.52	$159,028,000	0.66
FBR Ashton	1.15321	1.02805	85.47	$114,340,000	0.31
Keefe-Rainbow Partners	1.35679	1.11535	88.19	$112,160,000	0.41
Acadia Fund	1.00000	1.00000	215.50	$100,000,000	1.08
Caduceus Capital	1.02810	1.00000	349.27	$95,000,000	0.73
Dynamis Fund	1.19815	1.00000	271.75	$72,330,000	0.56
Financial Stocks	1.44176	1.13508	32.14	$71,467,000	0.11
Hangar 4 Eagle I	1.01889	1.00000	116.84	$70,700,000	0.51
Financial Edge Fund	1.42741	1.00000	242.92	$52,500,000	0.64
Crestwood Capital Intl	1.04274	1.04049	130.17	$40,471,000	0.52
Digital Century Capital	1.26184	1.03283	52.62	$40,000,000	0.26
Galleon Omni Technology Fund (A)	1.00000	1.00000	171.60	$39,000,000	0.66
America First Fin Institutions Invest.	1.21990	1.12888	67.46	$37,410,000	0.27
Polaris Prime Technology	1.09529	1.00000	269.20	$37,174,000	0.85

TABLE 6.17 Long Only Input-Oriented CRS and VRS Models

DMU Name	Input-Oriented CRS Efficiency	Benchmark	Input-Oriented VRS Efficiency	Benchmark
KR Capital Partners Fund I	0.45616	Rutledge Partners	0.61752	Marksman Partners
Hamton I–Bond 004 {Euro}	1.00000	Hamton I–Bond 004 {Euro}	1.00000	Hamton I–Bond 004 {Euro}
Zazove Aggressive Growth Fund	0.54691	Hamton I–Bond 004 {Euro}, Rutledge Partners	0.58997	Hamton I–Bond 004 {Euro}, Rutledge Partners
Rutledge Partners	1.00000	Rutledge Partners	1.00000	Rutledge Partners
Marksman Partners	0.91196	Hamton I–Bond 004 {Euro}, Rutledge Partners	1.00000	Marksman Partners

TABLE 6.18 Long Only Output-Oriented CRS and VRS Models

DMU Name	Output-Oriented CRS Efficiency	Output-Oriented VRS Efficiency	Compounded Return	Dollars Under Management	Annualized Sharpe Ratio
KR Capital Partners Fund I	2.19221	2.06318	34.31	$98,658,000	0.10
Hamton I–Bond 004 {Euro}	1.00000	1.00000	163.90	$68,740,000	0.56
Zazove Aggressive Growth Fund	1.82844	1.18445	221.40	$46,400,000	0.56
Rutledge Partners	1.00000	1.00000	290.32	$18,105,000	0.52
Marksman Partners	1.09654	1.00000	95.89	$10,600,000	0.36

TABLE 6.19 Short Sellers Input-Oriented CRS and VRS Models

DMU Name	Input-Oriented CRS Efficiency	Benchmark	Input-Oriented VRS Efficiency	Benchmark
Permal US Opportunities	1.00000	Permal Us Opportunities	1.00000	Permal US Opportunities
Arcas Intl Fund (Covered Interests)	0.60846	C&O Investment Partnership	0.94961	C&O Investment Partnership, Arcas Covered Fund
C&O Investment Partnership	1.00000	C&O Investment Partnership	1.00000	C&O Investment Partnership
Arcas Fund II (Covered Interests)	0.62553	C&O Investment Partnership	0.99039	C&O Investment Partnership, Arcas Covered Fund
Arcas Covered Fund	0.60369	C&O Investment Partnership	1.00000	Arcas Covered Fund

TABLE 6.20 Short Sellers Output-Oriented CRS and VRS Models

DMU Name	Output-Oriented CRS Efficiency	Output-Oriented VRS Efficiency	Compounded Return	Dollars Under Management	Annualized Sharpe Ratio
Permal US Opportunities	1.00000	1.00000	141.34	$519,000,000	0.59
Arcas Intl Fund (Covered Interests)	1.64348	1.03145	6.51	$90,000,000	0.13
C&O Investment Partnership	1.00000	1.00000	90.11	$65,900,000	0.33
Arcas Fund II (Covered Interests)	1.59864	1.00583	4.67	$15,000,000	0.13
Arcas Covered Fund	1.65647	1.00000	1.89	$12,000,000	0.16

TABLE 6.21 Diversified CTA Input-Oriented CRS and VRS Models

DMU Name	Input-Oriented CRS Efficiency	Benchmark	Input-Oriented VRS Efficiency	Benchmark
Astmax Co (Genesis)	1.00000	Astmax Co (Genesis)	1.00000	Astmax Co (Genesis)
Astmax Co (Prelude)	0.90808	Grinham Managed Funds PTY	0.91506	Grinham Managed Funds PTY, Winton Capital Mgt
Sunrise Capital (Expanded Diversified)	0.98062	Grinham Managed Funds PTY	0.99411	Grinham Managed Funds PTY, Beach Capital Mgt (Discretionary), Winton Capital Mgt
Crabel Capital Mgt (Div Fut Unlev)	1.00000	Crabel Capital Mgt (Div Fut Unlev)	1.00000	Crabel Capital Mgt (Div Fut Unlev)
Rotella Capital (Standard Lev)	0.93252	Grinham Managed Funds PTY, Beach Capital Mgt (Discretionary)	0.93636	Grinham Managed Funds Pty, Beach Capital Mgt (Discretionary), Winton Capital Mgt
Grinham Managed Funds PTY	1.00000	Grinham Managed Funds PTY	1.00000	Grinham Managed Funds Pty
John W Henry & Co (Strat Allocation)	0.93683	Grinham Managed Funds PTY	1.00000	John W Henry & Co (Strat Allocation)
Beach Capital Mgt (Discretionary)	1.00000	Beach Capital Mgt (Discretionary)	1.00000	Beach Capital Mgt (Discretionary)
Graham Capital Mgt (GDP)	0.95716	Grinham Managed Funds PTY	0.96747	Grinham Managed Funds PTY, Beach Capital Mgt (Discretionary), Winton Capital Mgt

TABLE 6.21 (Continued)

DMU Name	Input-Oriented CRS Efficiency	Benchmark	Input-Oriented VRS Efficiency	Benchmark
Transtrend (Enhanced Risk USD)	1.00000	Transtrend (Enhanced Risk USD)	1.00000	Transtrend (Enhanced Risk USD)
RG Niederhoffer Capital Mgt	0.90234	Grinham Managed Funds PTY	1.00000	RG Niederhoffer Capital Mgt
Winton Capital Mgt	1.00000	Winton Capital Mgt	1.00000	Winton Capital Mgt
Millburn Ridgefield (Diversified)	0.83310	Grinham Managed Funds PTY	0.86704	Grinham Managed Funds PTY, John W Henry & Co (Strat Allocation), Beach Capital Mgt (Discretionary)
First Quadrant (Managed Futures)	0.66739	Grinham Managed Funds PTY	1.00000	First Quadrant (Managed Futures)
Campbell & Co (GL/Diversified Large)	0.90705	Grinham Managed Funds PTY, Beach Capital Mgt (Discretionary)	0.94709	Crabel Capital Mgt (Div Fut Unlev), Grinham Managed Funds PTY, Beach Capital Mgt (Discretionary)
Rabar Market Research	0.82944	Grinham Managed Funds PTY	0.86365	Grinham Managed Funds PTY, John W Henry & Co (Strat Allocation), Beach Capital Mgt (Discretionary)
Drury Capital (Diversified)	0.84057	Crabel Capital Mgt (Div Fut Unlev), Beach Capital Mgt (Discretionary)	0.87249	Crabel Capital Mgt (Div Fut Unlev), Beach Capital Mgt (Discretionary)
Cipher Investment Mgt	0.97314	Grinham Managed Funds PTY	0.98363	Grinham Managed Funds Pty, Beach Capital Mgt (Discretionary), Winton Capital Mgt
Eckhardt Trading (Standard)	1.00000	Eckhardt Trading (Standard)	1.00000	Eckhardt Trading (Standard)
Sunrise Capital (Diversified)	0.95278	Grinham Managed Funds PTY	0.96637	Grinham Managed Funds PTY, Beach Capital Mgt (Discretionary), Winton Capital Mgt

TABLE 6.22 Diversified CTA Output-Oriented CRS and VRS Models

DMU Name	Output-Oriented CRS Efficiency	Output-Oriented VRS Efficiency	Compounded Return	Dollars Under Management	Annualized Sharpe Ratio
Astmax Co (Genesis)	1.00000	1.00000	7.84	$2,093,553,000	−0.86
Astmax Co (Prelude)	1.10122	1.09134	50.75	$2,086,667,000	0.17
Sunrise Capital (Expanded Diversified)	1.01976	1.00510	121.30	$1,673,414,000	0.59
Crabel Capital Mgt (Div Fut Unlev)	1.00000	1.00000	51.65	$1,617,723,000	0.28
Rotella Capital (Standard Lev)	1.07236	1.05443	96.41	$1,528,300,000	0.49
Grinham Managed Funds Pty	1.00000	1.00000	66.91	$1,230,000,000	0.35
John W Henry & Co (Strat Allocation)	1.06743	1.00000	57.06	$1,212,964,000	0.2
Beach Capital Mgt (Discretionary)	1.00000	1.00000	271.19	$1,208,027,000	0.98
Graham Capital Mgt (GDP)	1.04476	1.02918	82.82	$1,185,400,000	0.36
Transtrend (Enhanced Risk USD)	1.00000	1.00000	129.15	$1,011,000,000	0.65
RG Niederhoffer Capital Mgt	1.10823	1.00000	97.58	$985,857,000	0.37
Winton Capital Mgt	1.00000	1.00000	179.82	$739,400,000	0.60
Millburn Ridgefield (Diversified)	1.20034	1.12012	18.90	$690,607,000	−0.04
First Quadrant (Managed Futures)	1.49837	1.00000	20.87	$672,588,000	−0.01
Campbell & Co (GL/Diversified Large)	1.10247	1.03679	95.18	$562,000,000	0.46
Rabar Market Research	1.20563	1.11722	56.66	$487,338,000	0.2
Drury Capital (Diversified)	1.18967	1.12422	203.19	$484,038,000	0.69
Cipher Investment Mgt	1.02760	1.01452	97.10	$460,000,000	0.43
Eckhardt Trading (Standard)	1.00000	1.00000	79.59	$390,008,000	0.34
Sunrise Capital (Diversified)	1.04956	1.03031	103.24	$339,456,000	0.46

TABLE 6.23 Financials CTA Input-Oriented CRS and VRS Models

DMU Name	Input-Oriented CRS Efficiency	Benchmark	Input-Oriented VRS Efficiency	Benchmark
Campbell & Co (Fin/Met/En Large)	0.91513	John W Henry & Co (Fin & Metals), Allied Irish Capital Mgt (Worldwide)	0.95369	John W Henry & Co (Fin & Metals), Cornerstone Trading (Intl Value), Allied Irish Capital Mgt (Worldwide)
Dunn Capital Mgt (WMA)	0.80602	John W Henry & Co (Fin & Metals), Cornerstone Trading (Intl Value), Allied Irish Capital Mgt (Worldwide)	1.00000	Dunn Capital Mgt (WMA)
Eclipse Capital (Global Monetary)	0.77756	Allied Irish Capital Mgt (Worldwide)	0.79715	John W Henry & Co (Fin & Metals), Cornerstone Trading (Intl Value), Allied Irish Capital Mgt (Worldwide)
Dunn Capital Mgt (Tops)	0.90796	Cornerstone Trading (Intl Value), Allied Irish Capital Mgt (Worldwide)	1.00000	Dunn Capital Mgt (Tops)
Capital Fund Mgt (Discus)	0.90673	John W Henry & Co (Fin & Metals), Allied Irish Capital Mgt (Worldwide)	0.93558	John W Henry & Co (Fin & Metals), Cornerstone Trading (Intl Value), Allied Irish Capital Mgt (Worldwide)
John W Henry & Co (Fin & Metals)	1.00000	John W Henry & Co (Fin & Metals)	1.00000	John W Henry & Co (Fin & Metals)
Campbell & Co (FME Small) Above $5M	0.87795	John W Henry & Co (Fin & Metals), Allied Irish Capital Mgt (Worldwide)	0.90761	John W Henry & Co (Fin & Metals), Cornerstone Trading (Intl Value), Allied Irish Capital Mgt (Worldwide)

Program				
Cornerstone Trading (Intl Value)	1.00000	Cornerstone Trading (Intl Value)	1.00000	Cornerstone Trading (Intl Value)
Eckhardt Trading (Global Financial)	0.86169	John W Henry & Co (Fin & Metals), Appleton Capital (Global Fin)	0.91771	John W Henry & Co (Fin & Metals), Cornerstone Trading (Intl Value), Appleton Capital (Global Fin)
Allied Irish Capital Mgt (Worldwide)	1.00000	Allied Irish Capital Mgt (Worldwide)	1.00000	Allied Irish Capital Mgt (Worldwide)
Sunrise Capital (Financials-Cimco)	0.87698	John W Henry & Co (Fin & Metals), Allied Irish Capital Mgt (Worldwide)	0.89776	John W Henry & Co (Fin & Metals), Cornerstone Trading (Intl Value), Allied Irish Capital Mgt (Worldwide)
John W Henry & Co (Global Fin & En)	0.78538	Allied Irish Capital Mgt (Worldwide)	0.85064	Dunn Capital Mgt (Tops), John W Henry & Co (Fin & Metals), Allied Irish Capital Mgt (Worldwide)
Marathon Capital (Financial)	0.90206	John W Henry & Co (Fin & Metals), Cornerstone Trading (Intl Value), Appleton Capital (Global Fin)	0.92080	John W Henry & Co (Fin & Metals), Cornerstone Trading (Intl Value), Appleton Capital (Global Fin)
IIU Breakout Program	0.87874	John W Henry & Co (Fin & Metals), Allied Irish Capital Mgt (Worldwide)	0.87920	John W Henry & Co (Fin & Metals), Allied Irish Capital Mgt (Worldwide)
Lyon Investment(Fin/Cur Contra Trend)	0.89903	John W Henry & Co (Fin & Metals), Allied Irish Capital Mgt (Worldwide)	0.90822	John W Henry & Co (Fin & Metals), Allied Irish Capital Mgt (Worldwide)

TABLE 6.23 (*Continued*)

DMU Name	Input-Oriented CRS Efficiency	Benchmark	Input-Oriented VRS Efficiency	Benchmark
Millburn Ridgefield (Global Financial)	0.83076	John W Henry & Co (Fin & Metals), Allied Irish Capital Mgt (Worldwide)	0.83823	John W Henry & Co (Fin & Metals), Allied Irish Capital Mgt (Worldwide)
Smith Point Invest (Regular)	0.96233	John W Henry & Co (Fin & Metals), Allied Irish Capital Mgt (Worldwide)	0.98527	John W Henry & Co (Fin & Metals), Cornerstone Trading (Intl Value), Allied Irish Capital Mgt (Worldwide)
Viguerie Investments	0.88118	John W Henry & Co (Fin & Metals), Allied Irish Capital Mgt (Worldwide)	0.89195	John W Henry & Co (Fin & (Intl Metals), Cornerstone Trading Value), Allied Irish Capital Mgt (Worldwide)
Appleton Capital (Global Fin)	1.00000	Appleton Capital (Global Fin)	1.00000	Appleton Capital (Global Fin)
Ashley Capital Mgt	0.83456	John W Henry & Co (Fin & Metals), Allied Irish Capital Mgt (Worldwide)	0.84993	John W Henry & Co (Fin & Metals), Cornerstone Trading (Intl Value), Allied Irish Capital Mgt (Worldwide)

TABLE 6.24 Financials CTA Output-Oriented CRS and VRS Models

DMU Name	Output-Oriented CRS Efficiency	Output-Oriented VRS Efficiency	Compounded Return	Dollars Under Management	Annualized Sharpe Ratio
Campbell & Co (Fin/Met/En Large)	1.09274	1.02586	124.48	$7,009,200,000	0.61
Dunn Capital Mgt (WMA)	1.24066	1.00000	37.79	$625,943,000	0.19
Eclipse Capital (Global Monetary)	1.28608	1.14033	49.43	$476,843,000	0.16
Dunn Capital Mgt (Tops)	1.10137	1.00000	68.03	$473,627,000	0.26
Capital Fund Mgt (Discus)	1.10287	1.06783	87.67	$380,491,000	0.41
John W Henry & Co (Fin & Metals)	1.00000	1.00000	47.66	$337,595,000	0.17
Campbell & Co (FME Small) Above $5m	1.13902	1.04533	97.10	$328,400,000	0.47
Cornerstone Trading (Intl Value)	1.00000	1.00000	236.59	$328,000,000	1.01
Eckhardt Trading (Global Financial)	1.16050	1.08160	93.21	$269,112,000	0.43
Allied Irish Capital Mgt (Worldwide)	1.00000	1.00000	29.15	$194,000,000	-0.45
Sunrise Capital (Financials-Cimco)	1.14028	1.09247	48.17	$179,235,000	0.16
John W Henry & Co (Global Fin & En)	1.27327	1.05826	38.63	$31,015,000	0.15
Marathon Capital (Financial)	1.10857	1.07525	83.31	$20,153,000	0.37
IIU Breakout Program	1.13800	1.13461	30.85	$14,000,000	-0.06
Lyon Investment(Fin/Cur Contra Trend)	1.11231	1.09955	35.72	$13,000,000	0.05
Millburn Ridgefield (Global Financial)	1.20371	1.16434	5.56	$12,705,000	-0.14
Smith Point Invest (Regular)	1.03914	1.01474	75.45	$10,473,000	0.33
Viguerie Investments	1.13484	1.11911	42.41	$9,500,000	0.11
Appleton Capital (Global Fin)	1.00000	1.00000	25.85	$9,000,000	-0.37
Ashley Capital Mgt	1.19823	1.14053	67.75	$7,050,000	0.26

TABLE 6.25 Currency CTA Input-Oriented CRS and VRS Models

DMU Name	Input-Oriented CRS		Input-Oriented VRS	
	Efficiency	Benchmark	Efficiency	Benchmark
FX Concepts (Developed Markets Cur)	0.87694	Allied Irish Capital Mgt (Forex), Millburn Ridgefield (Currency)	1.00000	FX Concepts (Developed Markets Cur)
Quantitative Financial (IPS Currency)	0.86422	Allied Irish Capital Mgt (Forex), Coral Rock Investment (White Coral)	1.00000	Quantitative Financial (IPS Currency)
Allied Irish Capital Mgt (Forex)	1.00000	Allied Irish Capital Mgt (Forex)	1.00000	Allied Irish Capital Mgt (Forex)
IKOS (Currency)	0.84966	Allied Irish Capital Mgt (Forex), Millburn Ridgefield (Currency)	0.91880	Quantitative Financial (IPS Currency), Allied Irish Capital Mgt (Forex), C-View Ltd, Millburn Ridgefield (Currency)
Analytic Investment Mgt (N-LIN)	0.81816	Allied Irish Capital Mgt (Forex), Coral Rock Investment (White Coral)	0.82173	Allied Irish Capital Mgt (Forex), Millburn Ridgefield (Currency), Hathersage Capital (Daily Growth)
Sunrise Capital (Currency)	0.91383	Allied Irish Capital Mgt (Forex), Millburn Ridgefield (Currency), Hathersage Capital (Daily Growth)	0.91500	Allied Irish Capital Mgt (Forex), Millburn Ridgefield (Currency), Marathon Capital (System Fx), Hathersage Capital (Daily Growth)
John W Henry & Co (Intl FX)	0.84497	Allied Irish Capital Mgt (Forex), Millburn Ridgefield (Currency)	1.00000	John W Henry & Co (Intl FX)
C-View Ltd	1.00000	C-View Ltd	1.00000	C-View Ltd
Coral Rock Investment (White Coral)	1.00000	Coral Rock Investment (White Coral)	1.00000	Coral Rock Investment (White Coral)

Jacobson Fund Managers (2.5X Lev)	0.70972	Allied Irish Capital Mgt (Forex), Coral Rock Investment (White Coral)	0.80477	Quantitative Financial (IPS Currency), Allied Irish Capital Mgt (Forex), C-View Ltd, Millburn Ridgefield (Currency)
Appleton Capital (25% Risk)	0.73606	Allied Irish Capital Mgt (Forex), Millburn Ridgefield (Currency)	1.00000	Appleton Capital (25% Risk)
John W Henry & Co (G-7 Currency)	0.92710	Allied Irish Capital Mgt (Forex), Millburn Ridgefield (Currency)	1.00000	John W Henry & Co (G-7 Currency)
Jacobson Fund Managers (1.0X Lev)	0.71962	Allied Irish Capital Mgt (Forex), Coral Rock Investment (White Coral)	0.78738	Quantitative Financial (IPS Currency), Allied Irish Capital Mgt (Forex), C-View Ltd, Marathon Capital (System FX)
Hathersage Capital Mgt (Long-Term)	0.83157	Allied Irish Capital Mgt (Forex), Millburn Ridgefield (Currency), Hathersage Capital (Daily Growth)	1.00000	Hathersage Capital Mgt (Long-Term)
Compucom Finance	0.86383	Allied Irish Capital Mgt (Forex), Coral Rock Investment (White Coral), Hathersage Capital (Daily Growth)	1.00000	Compucom Finance
Appleton Capital (10% Risk)	0.79177	Allied Irish Capital Mgt (Forex), Millburn Ridgefield (Currency)	0.81696	Allied Irish Capital Mgt (Forex), C-View Ltd, Millburn Ridgefield (Currency)
Millburn Ridgefield (Currency)	1.00000	Millburn Ridgefield (Currency)	0.93904	Millburn Ridgefield (Currency)
Willowbridge Associates (Currency)	0.92345	Allied Irish Capital Mgt (Forex), Millburn Ridgefield (Currency)	1.00000	Quantitative Financial (IPS Currency), Allied Irish Capital Mgt (Forex), Millburn Ridgefield (Currency), Marathon Capital (System FX)
Marathon Capital (System FX)	0.94345	Allied Irish Capital Mgt (Forex), Millburn Ridgefield (Currency)	1.00000	Marathon Capital (System FX)
Hathersage Capital (Daily Growth)	1.00000	Hathersage Capital (Daily Growth)	1.00000	Hathersage Capital (Daily Growth)

TABLE 6.26 Currency CTA Output-Oriented CRS and VRS Models

DMU Name	Output-Oriented CRS Efficiency	Output-Oriented VRS Efficiency	Compounded Return	Dollars Under Management	Annualized Sharpe Ratio
FX Concepts (Developed Markets Cur)	1.14033	1.00000	76.10	$3,300,000,000,000	0.33
Quantitative Financial (IPS Currency)	1.15711	1.00000	108.79	$1,943,000,000,000	0.52
Allied Irish Capital Mgt (Forex)	1.00000	1.00000	33.76	$424,000,000	−0.15
IKOS (Currency)	1.17695	1.07431	50.61	$390,900,000	0.20
Analytic Investment Mgt (N-LIN)	1.22226	1.20974	18.50	$264,200,000	−0.64
Sunrise Capital (Currency)	1.09429	1.08058	32.40	$230,123,000	0.01
John W Henry & Co (Intl FX)	1.18347	1.00000	61.46	$200,061,000	0.22
C-View Ltd	1.00000	1.00000	55.33	$168,800,000	0.61
Coral Rock Investment (White Coral)	1.00000	1.00000	22.18	$136,500,000	−1.14
Jacobson Fund Managers (2.5x Lev)	1.40901	1.04785	86.48	$135,000,000	0.39
Appleton Capital (25% Risk)	1.35858	1.00000	57.57	$124,000,000	0.21
John W Henry & Co (G-7 Currency)	1.07864	1.00000	17.71	$75,460,000	0.00
Jacobson Fund Managers (1.0x Lev)	1.38962	1.14707	50.69	$75,000,000	0.26
Hathersage Capital Mgt (Long-Term)	1.20254	1.00000	85.77	$63,200,000	0.49
Compucom Finance	1.15763	1.00000	47.69	$53,000,000	0.15
Appleton Capital (10% Risk)	1.26299	1.16503	33.69	$42,000,000	−0.01
Millburn Ridgefield (Currency)	1.00000	1.00000	6.37	$35,623,000	−0.15
Willowbridge Associates (Currency)	1.08290	1.05709	19.43	$18,491,000	−0.07
Marathon Capital (System FX)	1.05994	1.00000	49.69	$15,495,000	0.21
Hathersage Capital (Daily Growth)	1.00000	1.00000	124.31	$13,000,000	0.74

TABLE 6.27 Stock Index CTA Input-Oriented CRS and VRS Models

DMU Name	Input-Oriented CRS Efficiency	Benchmark	Input-Oriented VRS Efficiency	Benchmark
Ansbacher Investment Mgt	0.77095	Analytic Investment Mgt (IFT), Michael N Trading (FFTP), Strategic Investments (Equity Hedge)	0.79762	Oxeye Capital Mgt (Fut & Opt), Michael N Trading (FFTP), Strategic Investments (Equity Hedge)
Analytic Investment Mgt (IFT)	1.00000	Analytic Investment Mgt (IFT)	1.00000	Analytic Investment Mgt (IFT)
Oxeye Capital Mgt (Fut & Opt)	0.93900	Michael N Trading (FFTP), Strategic Investments (Equity Hedge)	1.00000	Oxeye Capital Mgt (Fut & Opt)
Michael N Trading (FFTP)	1.00000	Michael N Trading (FFTP)	1.00000	Michael N Trading (FFTP)
Strategic Investments (Equity Hedge)	1.00000	Strategic Investments (Equity Hedge)	1.00000	Strategic Investments (Equity Hedge)
Witter & Lester (Intermediate)	0.87817	Analytic Investment Mgt (IFT), Michael N Trading (FFTP), Strategic Investments (Equity Hedge)	0.97176	Allied Irish Capital Mgt (Equity Index)
Stan Udler (Global Index Program)	0.95648	Analytic Investment Mgt (IFT), Michael N Trading (FFTP), Strategic Investments (Equity Hedge)	0.95739	Analytic Investment Mgt (IFT), Michael N Trading (FFTP), Strategic Investments (Equity Hedge), Witter & Lester (Redstone)

TABLE 6.27 *(Continued)*

DMU Name	Input-Oriented CRS Efficiency	Benchmark	Input-Oriented VRS Efficiency	Benchmark
Allied Irish Capital Mgt (Equity Index)	1.00000	Allied Irish Capital Mgt (Equity Index)	1.00000	Allied Irish Capital Mgt (Equity Index)
Witter & Lester (Redstone)	1.00000	Witter & Lester (Redstone)	1.00000	Witter & Lester (Redstone)
Witter & Lester (Stock Index)	0.78520	Analytic Investment Mgt (IFT), Strategic Investments (Equity Hedge)	0.80029	Michael N Trading (FFTP), Strategic Investments (Equity Hedge), Witter & Lester (Redstone)
Intl Trading Advisors (Index)	0.91064	Michael N Trading (FFTP), Strategic Investments (Equity Hedge)	1.00000	Intl Trading Advisors (Index)

TABLE 6.28 Stock Index CTA Output-Oriented CRS and VRS Models

DMU Name	Output-Oriented CRS Efficiency	Output-Oriented VRS Efficiency	Compounded Return	Dollars Under Management	Annualized Sharpe Ratio
Ansbacher Investment Mgt	1.29711	1.11932	147.99	$81,500,000	0.53
Analytic Investment Mgt (Ift)	1.00000	1.00000	13.65	$50,190,000	-0.65
Oxeye Capital Mgt (Fut & Opt)	1.06496	1.00000	3,786.48	$37,600,000	1.45
Michael N Trading (FFTP)	1.00000	1.00000	556.09	$34,900,000	1.61
Strategic Investments (Equity Hedge)	1.00000	1.00000	85.99	$10,500,000	0.40
Witter & Lester (Intermediate)	1.13873	1.02007	20.26	$10,186,000	-0.23
Stan Udler (Global Index Program)	1.04550	1.04105	215.07	$7,742,000	0.93
Allied Irish Capital Mgt (Equity Index)	1.00000	1.00000	17.27	$4,000,000	-0.57
Witter & Lester (Redstone)	1.00000	1.00000	43.54	$1,834,000	0.16
Witter & Lester (Stock Index)	1.27356	1.23089	47.63	$754,000	0.15
Intl Trading Advisors (Index)	1.09812	1.00000	20.12	$346,000	-0.01

TABLE 6.29 Agricultural CTA Input-Oriented CRS and VRS Models

DMU Name	Input-Oriented CRS Efficiency	Benchmark	Input-Oriented VRS Efficiency	Benchmark
Yutaka Futures Co (Arbitrage)	0.45507	Strategic Investments (Agriculture)	1.00000	Yutaka Futures Co (Arbitrage)
Range Wise	0.73530	Strategic Investments (Agriculture)	0.79375	Yutaka Futures Co (Arbitrage), Strategic Investments (Agriculture)
Agtech Trading Company	0.58933	Strategic Investments (Agriculture)	1.00000	Agtech Trading Company
Kottke Associates (Crush)	0.44196	Strategic Investments (Agriculture)	0.81738	Yutaka Futures Co (Arbitrage), Strategic Investments (Agriculture)
Strategic Investments (Agriculture)	1.00000	Strategic Investments (Agriculture)	1.00000	Strategic Investments (Agriculture)

TABLE 6.30 Agricultural CTA Output-Oriented CRS and VRS Models

DMU Name	Output-Oriented CRS Efficiency	Output-Oriented VRS Efficiency	Compounded Return	Dollars Under Management	Annualized Sharpe Ratio
Yutaka Futures Co (Arbitrage)	2.19748	1.00000	39.98	$2,212,019,000	0.08
Range Wise	1.35999	1.12392	111.03	$30,277,000	0.42
Agtech Trading Company	1.69684	1.00000	91.28	$944,000	0.32
Kottke Associates (Crush)	2.26267	2.17860	24.14	$500,000	−0.05
Strategic Investments (Agriculture)	1.00000	1.00000	149.12	$100,000	0.52

TABLE 6.31 Spearman Correlation of Hedge Fund and CTA Classifications

DMU Name	Input-Oriented CRS-VRS Efficiency	Output-Oriented CRS-VRS Efficiency
	Hedge Funds	
Fund of Hedge Funds	0.906** (<.0001)	0.823** (<.0001)
Event Driven	0.917** (<.0001)	0.690** (.001)
Market Neutral	0.361 (.118)	0.210 (.373)
Global Macro	0.941** (<.0001)	0.788** (.001)
Global Emerging	0.412 (.071)	0.720 (.769)
Global Established	0.512* (.021)	0.485* (.030)
Global International	0.910** (<.0001)	0.790** (<.0001)
Sector	0.689** (.001)	0.665** (.001)
Long Only	0.803 (.102)	0.918* (.028)
Short Sellers	0.344 (0.571)	0.344 (.571)
	CTAs	
Diversified	0.644** (.002)	0.637** (.003)
Financial	0.770** (<.0001)	0.655** (.002)
Currency	0.604** (.005)	0.528* (.017)
Stock Index	0.784** (.004)	0.773** (.005)
Agricultural	0.112 (.858)	0.447 (.450)

*significant at the 0.05 level (1-tailed)
**significant at the 0.01 level (1-tailed)

CONCLUSION

Hedge fund managers, FOF managers, and CTAs must often change their exposure to risk and leverage in response to changing economic and market conditions. If the environment dictates no risk, a CRS model may be appropriate for selecting a fund because an equal amount of standard deviation (input) may result in an equal amount of return (output). However, the VRS model may be a better choice if the market is expected to rise. Under this condition, an input such as leverage may provide a greater amount of output (return).

Investors and FOF managers must determine whether an input- or output-oriented model is best suited for the current market environment, and what fits best with the appropriate hedge fund or CTA strategy. Because of their low volatility, market-neutral or event-driven funds may be best screened by using a CRS model, while the VRS model may be better suited for global macro funds because of their considerable use of leverage.

Investors can also use the various input and output models during different subperiods, or they may even prefer to adopt a longer time frame to compare fund results during short and long periods. Furthermore, the stability of hedge funds and CTAs can be examined during bull and bear markets to observe efficiency during both periods. Hedge fund managers, FOF managers, and CTAs may also use these various models to examine the internal efficiency of their own fund when using different input and output variables.

CHAPTER 7

Application of Returns-to-Scale

INTRODUCTION

In the previous chapter, we examined the input and output CRS and VRS models. If we now assume that hedge fund managers or CTAs can produce greater returns in proportion to their inputs, then they are operating under increasing returns-to-scale. In other words, returns increase if a hedge fund manager or CTA increases leverage. If too much leverage (an input) is used, then liquidating positions may result in decreasing returns-to-scale.

A hedge fund manager or CTA under constant returns-to-scale can scale their inputs and outputs in a linear manner without increasing or decreasing efficiency. Under this scenario, the fund can obtain a proportional output with a proportional amount of input. Returns-to-scale (RTS) can be either increasing, decreasing, or constant. In essence, the efficiency scores obtained from the inputs and outputs are the same. However, when varying returns-to-scale exist, inputs and outputs are different. Thus, when inputs are increased, outputs may change.

Returns-to-scale is important for fund selection because it is based on increasing or decreasing efficiency and on the asset size of the fund. Increasing returns-to-scale implies that increasing the risk of a hedge fund by 5% would result in increasing the returns by 10%, and vice versa. Constant RTS indicates that doubling inputs will exactly double the outputs. Decreasing RTS implies that doubling the inputs will less than double the outputs, and increasing RTS means that doubling the inputs will more than double the outputs.

TABLE 7.1   RTS Regions

Region I	Increasing Returns-to-Scale (IRS)
Region II	Constant Returns-to-Scale (CRS)
Region III	Decreasing Returns-to-Scale (DRS)
Region IV	IRS (input-oriented) and CRS (output-oriented)
Region V	CRS (input-oriented) and DRS (output-oriented)
Region VI	IRS (input-oriented) and DRS (output-oriented)

Wilkens and Zhu (2003) show how a "returns-to-scale" estimation technique in DEA can be used to classify hedge funds using the Centre for International Securities and Derivatives Markets (CISDM) indices. The authors conclude that DEA is a valid technique for classifying hedge funds (see more discussion in Chapter 3).

The RTS regions produced in DEA can be compared to the factor analysis technique used by Fung and Hsieh (1997), and the general style classification (GSC) system used by Brown and Goetzmann (1997, 2001), which generates five to eight distinct fund groups. Hedge fund and CTA classifications used by database vendors are not very accurate and not well defined because the styles are based on information provided by hedge fund managers and CTAs themselves. As Brown and Goetzmann (2001) note, this may result in incorrect self-classification.

These strategies are highly correlated to the self-reported style information groupings of hedge fund managers and CTAs. RTS can play an important role in manager selection by grouping the individual funds into the appropriate RTS regions.

Table 7.1 presents the six different RTS regions.

RESULTS

Table 7.2 shows that the RTS methodology creates four distinct groups of funds (Region II, Region III, Region V, and Region VI). Ironwood Partners and DKR International Relative Value (A) fall into Region II. These funds produce constant returns-to-scale according to the inputs and outputs we selected at the outset.

In Region III, six funds experience decreasing returns-to-scale (Meridian Horizon Fund, Mesirow Event Strategies Fund, Momentum All-

TABLE 7.2 Fund of Hedge Funds RTS Mode

DMU Name	RTS Region
GAM Diversity Fund	Region VI
Permal Investment Holdings NV (A)	Region VI
Haussman Holdings NV	Region VI
Mesirow Alternative Strategies Fund	Region V
JP Morgan Multi-Strategy Fund	Region VI
Man-Glenwood Multi-Strategy Fund	Region VI
Coast Diversified Fund	Region VI
Aurora	Region VI
Lighthouse Diversified Fund	Region VI
Mesirow Equity Opportunity Fund	Region VI
Meridian Horizon Fund	Region III
Leveraged Capital Holdings	Region VI
Ironwood Partners	Region II
Dkr Intl Relative Value (A)	Region II
Mesirow Event Strategies Fund	Region III
Momentum Allweather Fund	Region III
Green Way Class B {Euro}	Region VI
Edison Fund Class A	Region III
Permal Japan Holdings	Region III
Asian Capital Holdings Fund	Region III

Weather Fund, Edison Fund Class (A), Permal Japan Holdings, and Asian Capital Holdings Ltd.). In Region V, the Mesirow Alternative Strategies Fund is the only fund that produces CRS (input-oriented) and DRS (output-oriented). Region VI contains the remaining 11 funds that experience IRS (input-oriented) and DRS (output-oriented).

RTS benefits investors and FOF managers by grouping funds into their specific regions, just as factor analysis and GSC are frequently used to group hedge funds, FOFs, and CTAs. A FOF manager may use both of these techniques for comparison purposes and to provide a complementary technique for hedge fund manager and CTA selection.

For Tables 7.3 through 7.16, the same analysis can be applied to the remaining hedge fund and CTA classifications.

TABLE 7.3 Event-Driven RTS Model

DMU Name	RTS Region
King Street Capital Ltd	Region II
Elliott Intl	Region VI
Canyon Value Realization Cayman (A)	Region VI
Elliott Associates	Region VI
York Investment	Region VI
King Street Capital	Region II
Paulson Intl	Region VI
Canyon Value Realization Cayman (B)	Region VI
Canyon Value Realization Fund	Region VI
Halcyon Offshore Event-Driven Strat	Region VI
York Select	Region III
York Capital Mgt	Region VI
Caspian Capital Partners	Region II
Paulson Partners	Region VI
Halcyon Fund	Region VI
GAM Arbitrage	Region VI
Triage Capital Mgt	Region III
Gabelli Associates	Region VI
Corsair Capital Partners (CCA)	Region III
American Durham	Region VI

TABLE 7.4 Market-Neutral RTS Model

DMU Name	RTS Region
Derivative Arbitrage Fund {Yen}	Region VI
Ellington Composite	Region III
Millennium Intl	Region II
Shepherd Investments Intl	Region VI
Deephaven Market Neutral Fund Ltd	Region V
Alexandra Global Master Fund	Region II
Stark Investments	Region VI
III Fund Ltd	Region VI
III Global	Region VI
Ellington Overseas Partners	Region III
MBS Fund Gamma (O)	Region II
Alta Partners Ltd	Region II
Libertyview Plus Fund	Region VI
Deephaven Market Neutral Fund	Region V
Double Black Diamond	Region VI
St Albans Partners	Region VI
Mkt Neutral Equitized Strat Comp	Region VI
Concordia Capital (A)	Region III
Argent Classic Conv ARB(Bermuda) (A)	Region VI
Black Diamond	Region II

TABLE 7.5 Global Macro RTS Model

DMU Name	RTS Region
Vega Global Fund	Region II
UBS Currency Portfolio	Region VI
Gamut Investments	Region II
Global Undervalued Securities Fund	Region II
LCM GL Int Rate Hedged Fund (Opport)	Region I
CRG Partners LDC	Region VI
Permal Europe {Euro}	Region VI
Wexford Offshore Spectrum Fund	Region VI
Wexford Spectrum Fund	Region VI
Quadriga AG {Euro}	Region III
Peak Partners	Region VI
GAM Cross-Market	Region VI
Grossman Currency Fund	Region VI
Universal Bond Fund	Region VI

TABLE 7.6 Global Emerging RTS Model

DMU Name	RTS Region
Ashmore Emerg Markets Liquid Invest	Region III
Hermitage Fund (Worst Bid)	Region VI
Ashmore Local Currency Debt Port	Region III
LIM Asia Arbitrage Fund	Region II
GLS Offshore Global Opportunities	Region VI
Consulta Emerging Markets Debt	Region III
Firebird Republics Fund	Region VI
Firebird New Russia Fund	Region VI
Greylock Global Opportunity Fund	Region III
EK Asia Fund	Region VI
GLS Global Opportunities Fund	Region VI
Griffin East European Value {Euro}	Region VI
Tiedemann/Ayer Asian Growth	Region VI
Key Global Emerging Markets	Region VI
Firebird Fund	Region VI
Ashmore Russian Debt Portfolio	Region III
Tradewinds Russia Partners I	Region VI
Futurewatch	Region II
Post Communist Opportunities Fund	Region VI
Opportunity Fund Brazilian Hedge	Region VI

TABLE 7.7 Global Established RTS Model

DMU Name	RTS Region
Eureka Fund {Euro}	Region II
Eureka Fund	Region II
Cobalt Partners	Region II
Steel Partners II	Region VI
Adelphi Europe Fund (B) {Euro}	Region VI
Cobalt Offshore Fund	Region VI
Odey European {Euro}	Region I
First Eagle Fund NV	Region VI
Pegasus Fund {BP}	Region III
Libra Fund	Region III
Eagle Capital Partners	Region VI
AJR International (A)	Region VI
Amici Associates	Region VI
Cambrian Fund (A)	Region VI
Seminole Capital Partners	Region II
Everglades Partners	Region VI
Giano Capital {Euro}	Region VI
Adelphi Europe Fund (A)	Region VI
Bricoleur Offshore	Region VI
New Star Hedge Fund {BP}	Region VI

TABLE 7.8 Global International RTS Model

DMU Name	RTS Region
Orbis Global Equity	Region III
Orbis Optimal {US}	Region III
Orbis Leveraged {US}	Region III
Platinum Fund	Region III
Lazard Global Opportunities Ltd	Region III
Lazard Global Opportunities	Region III
IIU Convertible Fund	Region II
GAM Selection	Region VI
Equinox Partners	Region III
Glenrock Global Partners	Region VI
Glenrock Global Partners (BVI)	Region VI
Third Avenue Global Value Fund	Region III
Stewart Asian Holdings	Region I
Millburn Intl Stock Index Fund	Region VI
Polaris Prime Europe	Region II
Zazove Global Convertible Fund	Region VI
Aravis Clipper Fund	Region VI
Performance Partners	Region II

TABLE 7.9 Sector RTS Model

DMU Name	RTS Region
Sandler Associates	Region II
Spinner Global Technology Fund	Region III
Basswood Financial Partners	Region VI
Sandler Offshore	Region II
Caduceus Capital Ltd	Region III
KCM Biomedical	Region II
Malta Hedge Fund II	Region II
FBR Ashton	Region III
Keefe-Rainbow Partners	Region V
Acadia Fund	Region II
Caduceus Capital	Region III
Dynamis Fund	Region III
Financial Stocks	Region VI
Hangar 4 Eagle I	Region I
Financial Edge Fund	Region III
Crestwood Capital Intl	Region VI
Digital Century Capital	Region VI
Galleon Omni Technology Fund (A)	Region II
America First Fin Institutions Invest.	Region VI
Polaris Prime Technology	Region III

TABLE 7.10 Long Only RTS Model

DMU Name	RTS Region
KR Capital Partners Fund I	Region I
Hamton I–Bond 004 {Euro}	Region II
Zazove Aggressive Growth Fund	Region III
Rutledge Partners	Region II
Marksman Partners	Region I

TABLE 7.11   Short Sellers RTS Model

DMU Name	RTS Region
Permal US Opportunities	Region II
Arcas Intl Fund (Covered Interests)	Region III
C&O Investment Partnership	Region II
Arcas Fund II (Covered Interests)	Region III
Arcas Covered Fund	Region III

TABLE 7.12   Diversified CTA RTS Model

DMU Name	RTS Region
Astmax Co (Genesis)	Region II
Astmax Co (Prelude)	Region VI
Sunrise Capital (Expanded Diversified)	Region III
Crabel Capital Mgt (Div Fut Unlev)	Region II
Rotella Capital (Standard Lev)	Region VI
Grinham Managed Funds PTY	Region II
John W Henry & Co (Strat Allocation)	Region III
Beach Capital Mgt (Discretionary)	Region II
Graham Capital Mgt (GDP)	Region III
Transtrend (Enhanced Risk USD)	Region III
RG Niederhoffer Capital Mgt	Region III
Winton Capital Mgt	Region III
Millburn Ridgefield (Diversified)	Region III
First Quadrant (Managed Futures)	Region III
Campbell & Co (GL/Diversified Large)	Region III
Rabar Market Research	Region III
Drury Capital (Diversified)	Region III
Cipher Investment Mgt	Region VI
Eckhardt Trading (Standard)	Region III
Sunrise Capital (Diversified)	Region III

TABLE 7.13 Financials CTA RTS Model

DMU Name	RTS Region
Campbell & Co (Fin/Met/En Large)	Region III
Dunn Capital Mgt (WMA)	Region III
Eclipse Capital (Global Monetary)	Region VI
Dunn Capital Mgt (Tops)	Region III
Capital Fund Mgt (Discus)	Region VI
John W Henry & Co (Fin & Metals)	Region III
Campbell & Co (FME Small) Above $5M	Region III
Cornerstone Trading (Intl Value)	Region II
Eckhardt Trading (Global Financial)	Region III
Allied Irish Capital Mgt (Worldwide)	Region II
Sunrise Capital (Financials-Cimco)	Region VI
John W Henry & Co (Global Fin & En)	Region VI
Marathon Capital (Financial)	Region III
Iiu Breakout Program	Region VI
Lyon Investment(Fin/Cur Contra Trend)	Region VI
Millburn Ridgefield (Global Financial)	Region VI
Smith Point Invest (Regular)	Region VI
Viguerie Investments	Region VI
Appleton Capital (Global Fin)	Region II
Ashley Capital Mgt	Region VI

TABLE 7.14 Currency CTA RTS Model

DMU Name	RTS Region
FX Concepts (Developed Markets CUR)	Region III
Quantitative Financial (IPS Currency)	Region III
Allied Irish Capital Mgt (Forex)	Region II
Ikos (Currency)	Region III
Analytic Investment Mgt (N-LIN)	Region VI
Sunrise Capital (Currency)	Region VI
John W Henry & Co (Intl FX)	Region III
C-View Ltd	Region II
Coral Rock Investment (White Coral)	Region II
Jacobson Fund Managers (2.5x Lev)	Region III
Appleton Capital (25% Risk)	Region III
John W Henry & Co (G-7 Currency)	Region VI
Jacobson Fund Managers (1.0x Lev)	Region III
Hathersage Capital Mgt (Long-Term)	Region III
Compucom Finance	Region VI
Appleton Capital (10% Risk)	Region III
Millburn Ridgefield (Currency)	Region VI
Willowbridge Associates (Currency)	Region VI
Marathon Capital (System FX)	Region III
Hathersage Capital (Daily Growth)	Region II

TABLE 7.15   Stock Index CTA RTS Model

DMU Name	RTS Region
Ansbacher Investment Mgt	Region VI
Analytic Investment Mgt (IFT)	Region II
Oxeye Capital Mgt (Fut & Opt)	Region III
Michael N Trading (FFTP)	Region II
Strategic Investments (Equity Hedge)	Region VI
Witter & Lester (Intermediate)	Region III
Stan Udler (Global Index Program)	Region VI
Allied Irish Capital Mgt (Equity Index)	Region II
Witter & Lester (Redstone)	Region II
Witter & Lester (Stock Index)	Region III
Intl Trading Advisors (Index)	Region VI

TABLE 7.16   Agricultural CTA RTS Model

DMU Name	RTS Region
Yutaka Futures Co (Arbitrage)	Region I
Range Wise	Region VI
Agtech Trading Company	Region III
Kottke Associates (Crush)	Region VI
Strategic Investments (Agriculture)	Region II

CONCLUSION

Investors and FOF managers should determine which RTS methodology best fits their needs by deciding where their fund is located with respect to the RTS region. Using different inputs and outputs—such as the size of the fund, leverage, the number of trades placed, and so on—will place the fund in different regions. Comparing the Generalized Style Classification groupings and RTS methodology groupings may add further insight into the performance and behavior of hedge funds, funds of hedge funds and CTAs in bull and bear markets. Each RTS methodology will provide different results.

CHAPTER 8

Application of Context-Dependent DEA

INTRODUCTION

Context-dependent data envelopment analysis (CDEA) in Chapter 3 evaluates a set of hedge funds or CTAs against a specific framework. The evaluation framework represents an efficient frontier generated by the set of hedge funds or CTAs in a particular performance level. Context-dependent DEA measures 1) the relative attractiveness when hedge funds or CTAs displaying inferior performance are selected as the evaluation framework, and 2) the progress when hedge funds or CTAs displaying superior performance are selected as the evaluation framework. The tables throughout this chapter give the efficiency scores of funds based on the attractiveness model.

CDEA's main advantage lies in its versatility: the multiple inputs, outputs, and efficient incremental frontiers (or different levels of the "best practices" frontier) that the model can generate. In DEA, an efficient frontier is created by the efficient hedge funds or CTAs. Deleting inefficient funds does not change the efficient funds, nor does it change the efficient frontier. The only way the inefficiency scores can be altered is if the efficient frontier itself has changed.

For example, the performance of hedge funds or CTAs is based solely on the recognized efficient frontier. A hedge fund or CTA that lies on the first-level efficient frontier may be more striking or attractive than one on the second level. Within a DEA context, it is important to note whether there is relative appeal or attractiveness of a particular hedge fund or CTA when compared to its peers. The relative appeal of Fund X compared to Fund Y would depend on the presence or absence of a third option—for example, Fund Z (or a group of funds). Relative attractiveness is based on the assessment framework constructed from different funds.

In fact, a group of hedge funds or CTAs can be separated into various levels of efficient frontiers. If the original efficient frontier is removed, the remaining (inefficient) hedge funds or CTAs will form a second-level efficient frontier, a third-level efficient frontier, and so on, until there are no funds remaining. Each individual frontier presents an appraisal framework for measuring relative attractiveness. In other words, the third-level frontier serves as the appraisal framework for measuring the relative attractiveness of the first-level (original) frontier fund. Otherwise, performance of third-level efficient frontier funds can be measured with respect to the first- or second-level efficient frontier.

As we note, context-dependent DEA examines the relative attractiveness achieved when funds with inferior performance are selected as the appraisal framework. The existence or non-existence of the efficient frontier affects the improvement of funds on a different efficient frontier level. For example, when hedge funds or CTAs on one level are regarded as attaining equal performance, the measure of attractiveness can distinguish "identical performance" based on the same specific appraisal framework.

Using various inputs and outputs can play a role in the evaluation of a hedge fund's or CTA's efficiency. Investors can also give priority to risk measures to get more insight into fund performance. Here, judgment plays a vital role when measuring relative efficiency within a CDEA setting. Hedge fund manager or CTA values based on certain inputs and outputs can vary from investor to investor, depending on their risk/return framework. Investors, hedge fund managers, funds of hedge fund managers, and CTAs can use various inputs and outputs to examine how the efficiency frontier can change. They may also wish to use this technique to select their own set of specific criteria. For example, adding a certain input like skewness will show investors if the funds can control for skewness. If average recovery time is a greater concern, selecting this as an input would alter the efficiency ranking of each hedge fund or CTA.

CDEA is ideal when FOF managers are selecting hedge funds and CTAs for their portfolios. FOF managers usually create a first, second, and third tier of hedge funds or CTAs of best-performing funds. In many cases, if certain good-performing hedge funds or CTAs are closed to new capital, FOF managers may have to scramble to find alternate funds. Thus, having a second and third tier of good funds at their disposal can be critical.

CDEA makes it possible to appraise and rank hedge funds and CTAs in a risk/return framework without using indices. CDEA can classify hundreds of hedge funds, funds of hedge funds, and CTAs in a formal efficiency tiered system. If FOF managers prefer hedge funds and CTAs that will minimize volatility and maximize drawdown, CDEA can make it possible to isolate those funds. Or, if FOF managers need efficient hedge funds and CTAs that are not exposed to extraordinary gains or losses (kurtosis), by selecting kurtosis as one of the inputs, CDEA can produce different best practices frontiers with varying levels of this efficiency. CDEA models offer a useful tool for ranking efficient hedge funds and CTAs using various levels of efficient frontiers.

RESULTS

Table 8.1 displays the attractiveness model of the FOF classification when different efficient frontiers are selected as the evaluation contexts. Using

TABLE 8.1 Funds of Hedge Funds Using Context-Dependent DEA

Level 1 (CRS) DMU Name	Input-Oriented Level 2 (CRS) Context-Dependent Score	Benchmarks
Ironwood Partners	1.27156	Coast Diversified Fund
DKR Intl Relative Value (A)	1.76783	Coast Diversified Fund, Mesirow Equity Opportunity Fund
Permal Japan Holdings	1.21364	Edison Fund Class A

Level 1 (CRS) DMU Name	Input-Oriented Level 3 (CRS) Context-Dependent Score	Benchmarks
Ironwood Partners	1.39634	JP Morgan Multi-Strategy Fund, Meridian Horizon Fund
DKR Intl Relative Value (A)	2.50517	JP Morgan Multi-Strategy Fund
Permal Japan Holdings	1.41571	Meridian Horizon Fund, Asian Capital Holdings Fund

Level 2 (CRS) DMU Name	Input-Oriented Level 3 (CRS) Context-Dependent Score	Benchmarks
Coast Diversified Fund	1.19836	JP Morgan Multi-Strategy Fund, Mesirow Event Strategies Fund
Mesirow Equity Opportunity Fund	1.24290	JP Morgan Multi-Strategy Fund, Meridian Horizon Fund, Asian Capital Holdings Fund
Momentum All Weather Fund	1.09810	Mesirow Event Strategies Fund
Edison Fund Class A	1.85793	Meridian Horizon Fund

CDEA, we first obtain the number of levels before proceeding to the returns-to-scale analysis. We obtain six levels for the FOF classification according to *DEAFrontier*, of which three are used for demonstration purposes.

TABLE 8.2 Event Driven Using Context-Dependent DEA

Level 1 (CRS) DMU Name	Input-Oriented Level 2 (CRS) Context-Dependent Score	Benchmarks
King Street Capital Ltd	2.22122	Elliott Intl, Halcyon Fund
King Street Capital	2.41889	Elliott Intl, Halcyon Fund, Triage Capital Mgt
Caspian Capital Partners	3.51767	Elliott Associates

Level 1 (CRS) DMU Name	Input-Oriented Level 3 (CRS) Context-Dependent Score	Benchmarks
King Street Capital Ltd	2.85966	York Capital Mgt, American Durham
King Street Capital	3.33993	York Capital Mgt, American Durham
Caspian Capital Partners	4.77371	GAM Arbitrage, American Durham

Level 2 (CRS) DMU Name	Input-Oriented Level 3 (CRS) Context-Dependent Score	Benchmarks
Elliott Intl	1.43907	York Capital Mgt, GAM Arbitrage, American Durham
Elliott Associates	1.43890	York Capital Mgt, GAM Arbitrage, American Durham
Halcyon Offshore Event-Driven Strat	1.20045	York Capital Mgt, GAM Arbitrage, American Durham
Halcyon Fund	1.28719	York Capital Mgt, American Durham
Triage Capital Mgt	1.40108	York Capital Mgt, American Durham
Gabelli Associates	1.58137	GAM Arbitrage, American Durham

We use Level 1 (CRS), which consists of the funds to be evaluated against the selected context, and select Level 2 (CRS) as the evaluation background. We repeat the procedure with Level 3 (CRS) as the background. We also use Level 2 (CRS), which consists of the funds to be evaluated against the selected context Level 3 (CRS), and select Level 3 (CRS) as the evaluation background.

In Table 8.1, we find that using Level 1 with the background as Level 2 results in DKR International Relative Value (A) attaining the highest efficiency rating (1.767863). The benchmarks (or evaluation background) for DKR International Relative Value (A) are the Coast Diversified Fund and the Mesirow Equity Opportunity Fund. We find that using Level 1 with the background as Level 3 ranks DKR International Relative Value (A) as having the highest efficiency rating or context-dependent score (2.50517), with J. P. Morgan Multi-Strategy Fund as its respective benchmark (or evaluation background).

When examining Level 2 with the evaluation background as Level 3, Edison Fund Class (A) is ranked as the fund with the highest context-dependent score (1.85793). The respective benchmark is the Meridian Horizon Fund. A high attractiveness score denotes that the fund does not have a close competitor.

The same analysis can be applied for the remaining classifications in Tables 8.2 through 8.15.

TABLE 8.3   Market Neutral Using Context-Dependent DEA

Level 1 (CRS) DMU Name	Input-Oriented Level 2 (CRS) Context-Dependent Score	Benchmarks
Millennium Intl	2.61965	Deephaven Market Neutral Fund Ltd, Double Black Diamond
Alexandra Global Master Fund	3.03391	Double Black Diamond
MBS Fund Gamma (O)	1.19959	Libertyview Plus Fund, St Albans Partners
Alta Partners Ltd	3.03976	Double Black Diamond
Black Diamond	1.43052	Double Black Diamond, St Albans Partners

TABLE 8.3 *(Continued)*

Level 1 (CRS) DMU Name	Input-Oriented Level 3 (CRS) Context-Dependent Score	Benchmarks
Millennium Intl	3.14541	Deephaven Market Neutral Fund, Argent Classic Conv ARB (Bermuda) (A)
Alexandra Global Master Fund	3.34358	Deephaven Market Neutral Fund
MBS Fund Gamma (O)	5.81734	Derivative Arbitrage Fund {Yen}, Deephaven Market Neutral Fund
Alta Partners Ltd	6.17511	Deephaven Market Neutral Fund, Argent Classic Conv ARB(Bermuda) (A)
Black Diamond	4.60350	Derivative Arbitrage Fund {Yen}

Level 2 (CRS) DMU Name	Input-Oriented Level 3 (CRS) Context-Dependent Score	Benchmarks
Deephaven Market Neutral Fund Ltd	1.07626	Derivative Arbitrage Fund {Yen}, Deephaven Market Neutral Fund
Libertyview Plus Fund	2.06233	Derivative Arbitrage Fund {Yen}, Deephaven Market Neutral Fund
Double Black Diamond	2.40799	Derivative Arbitrage Fund {Yen}, Deephaven Market Neutral Fund, Argent Classic Conv ARB(Bermuda) (A)
St Albans Partners	2.81541	Derivative Arbitrage Fund {Yen}, Deephaven Market Neutral Fund
Concordia Capital (A)	1.74165	Deephaven Market Neutral Fund

TABLE 8.4 Global Macro Using Context-Dependent DEA

Level 1 (CRS) DMU Name	Input-Oriented Level 2 (CRS) Context-Dependent Score	Benchmarks
Vega Global Fund	2.58626	LCM GL Int Rate Hedged Fund (Opport)
Gamut Investments	2.18867	Wexford Offshore Spectrum Fund
Global Undervalued Securities Fund	1.53957	LCM Gl Int Rate Hedged Fund (Opport), GAM Cross-Market

Level 1 (CRS) DMU Name	Input-Oriented Level 3 (CRS) Context-Dependent Score	Benchmarks
Vega Global Fund	2.78517	UBS Currency Portfolio
Gamut Investments	3.13132	CRG Partners Ldc, Permal Europe {Euro}
Global Undervalued Securities Fund	2.01055	Permal Europe {Euro}

Level 2 (CRS) DMU Name	Input-Oriented Level 3 (CRS) Context-Dependent Score	Benchmarks
LCM GL Int Rate Hedged Fund (Opport)	1.36686	UBS Currency Portfolio, Permal Europe {Euro}
Wexford Offshore Spectrum Fund	1.46299	CRG Partners LDC, Permal Europe {Euro}
Wexford Spectrum Fund	1.45867	CRG Partners LDC, Permal Europe {Euro}
Quadriga AG {Euro}	1.10005	CRG Partners LDC, Permal Europe {Euro}, Grossman Currency Fund
Peak Partners	1.35829	CRG Partners LDC, Permal Europe {Euro}
GAM Cross-Market	1.76533	UBS Currency Portfolio, CRG Partners LDC, Permal Europe {Euro}

TABLE 8.5   Global International Using Context-Dependent DEA

Level 1 (CRS) DMU Name	Input-Oriented Level 2 (CRS) Context- Dependent Score	Benchmarks
Platinum Fund	1.47769	Orbis Optimal {US}, Orbis Leveraged {US}
IIU Convertible Fund	2.38076	Orbis Optimal {US}
Stewart Asian Holdings	1.70737	Orbis Leveraged {US}
Polaris Prime Europe	2.45397	Orbis Leveraged {US}
Performance Partners	1.64866	Orbis Optimal {US}

Level 1 (CRS) DMU Name	Input-Oriented Level 3 (CRS) Context- Dependent Score	Benchmarks
Platinum Fund	2.19041	Third Avenue Global Value Fund
IIU Convertible Fund	3.80485	Lazard Global Opportunities, Third Avenue Global Value Fund
Stewart Asian Holdings	2.26628	Third Avenue Global Value Fund
Polaris Prime Europe	3.25728	Third Avenue Global Value Fund
Performance Partners	2.70500	Lazard Global Opportunities

Level 2 (CRS) DMU Name	Input-Oriented Level 3 (CRS) Context- Dependent Score	Benchmarks
Orbis Optimal {US}	1.64072	Lazard Global Opportunities
Orbis Leveraged {US}	1.41169	Lazard Global Opportunities, Third Avenue Global Value Fund

TABLE 8.6   Global Emerging Using Context-Dependent DEA

Level 1 (CRS) DMU Name	Input-Oriented Level 2 (CRS) Context-Dependent Score	Benchmarks
LIM Asia Arbitrage Fund	2.81418	Greylock Global Opportunity Fund, EK Asia Fund
Futurewatch	2.62605	EK Asia Fund
Opportunity Fund Brazilian Hedge	1.53572	EK Asia Fund

Level 1 (CRS) DMU Name	Input-Oriented Level 3 (CRS) Context-Dependent Score	Benchmarks
LIM Asia Arbitrage Fund	4.80477	Ashmore Emerg Markets Liquid Invest, Tiedemann/Ayer Asian Growth
Futurewatch	6.67254	Ashmore Emerg Markets Liquid Invest, Griffin East European Value {Euro}
Opportunity Fund Brazilian Hedge	3.39759	Ashmore Emerg Markets Liquid Invest, Griffin East European Value {Euro}, Tiedemann/Ayer Asian Growth

Level 2 (CRS) DMU Name	Input-Oriented Level 3 (CRS) Context-Dependent Score	Benchmarks
Ashmore Local Currency Debt Port	1.26273	Consulta Emerging Markets Debt, Key Global Emerging Markets
Greylock Global Opportunity Fund	1.37375	Consulta Emerging Markets Debt, Tiedemann/Ayer Asian Growth
EK Asia Fund	2.71758	Ashmore Emerg Markets Liquid Invest, Griffin East European Value {Euro}, Tiedemann/Ayer Asian Growth
Ashmore Russian Debt Portfolio	1.15009	Consulta Emerging Markets Debt, Key Global Emerging Markets
Post Communist Opportunities Fund	1.56987	Griffin East European Value {Euro}, Key Global Emerging Markets

TABLE 8.7   Global Established Using Context-Dependent DEA

Level 1 (CRS) DMU Name	Input-Oriented Level 2 (CRS) Context-Dependent Score	Benchmarks
Eureka Fund {Euro}	2.92874	Adelphi Europe Fund (B) {Euro}, Odey European {Euro}, New Star Hedge Fund {BP}
Eureka Fund	3.17145	Adelphi Europe Fund (B) {Euro}, New Star Hedge Fund {BP}
Cobalt Partners	1.08086	Cobalt Offshore Fund, New Star Hedge Fund {BP}
Amici Associates	1.07691	Cobalt Offshore Fund, Odey European {Euro}, New Star Hedge Fund {BP}
Seminole Capital Partners	1.30036	Adelphi Europe Fund (B) {Euro}, Cobalt Offshore Fund, Pegasus Fund {BP}

Level 1 (CRS) DMU Name	Input-Oriented Level 3 (CRS) Context-Dependent Score	Benchmarks
Eureka Fund {Euro}	4.20923	Libra Fund, Bricoleur Offshore
Eureka Fund	4.58107	Libra Fund, Bricoleur Offshore
Cobalt Partners	1.42805	Eagle Capital Partners, Everglades Partners
Amici Associates	1.26884	Libra Fund, Eagle Capital Partners, Bricoleur Offshore
Seminole Capital Partners	1.90263	Giano Capital {Euro}

Level 2 (CRS) DMU Name	Input-Oriented Level 3 (CRS) Context-Dependent Score	Benchmarks
Steel Partners II	1.22720	Libra Fund, Giano Capital {Euro}, Bricoleur Offshore
Adelphi Europe Fund (B) {Euro}	1.64237	Giano Capital {Euro}
Cobalt Offshore Fund	1.34303	Eagle Capital Partners, Everglades Partners
Odey European {Euro}	1.38247	Libra Fund, Bricoleur Offshore
Pegasus Fund {BP}	1.43881	Everglades Partners, Giano Capital {Euro}
Adelphi Europe Fund (A)	1.54511	Giano Capital {Euro}
New Star Hedge Fund {BP}	1.46658	Libra Fund, Giano Capital {Euro}, Bricoleur Offshore

TABLE 8.8   Sector Using Context-Dependent DEA

Level 1 (CRS) DMU Name	Input-Oriented Level 2 (CRS) Context-Dependent Score	Benchmarks
Sandler Associates	1.97811	Caduceus Capital, Hangar 4 Eagle I, Polaris Prime Technology
Spinner Global Technology Fund	1.13158	Caduceus Capital, Hangar 4 Eagle I, Crestwood Capital Intl, Polaris Prime Technology
Sandler Offshore	1.89177	Caduceus Capital, Polaris Prime Technology
KCM Biomedical	1.09756	Hangar 4 Eagle I
Malta Hedge Fund II	1.77445	Basswood Financial Partners, Hangar 4 Eagle I
Acadia Fund	1.56350	Basswood Financial Partners, Polaris Prime Technology
Galleon Omni Technology Fund (A)	1.12155	Caduceus Capital, Hangar 4 Eagle I, Polaris Prime Technology

Level 1 (CRS) DMU Name	Input-Oriented Level 3 (CRS) Context-Dependent Score	Benchmarks
Sandler Associates	2.78949	Sandler Associates, Caduceus Capital Ltd, America First Fin Institutions Invest
Spinner Global Technology Fund	1.38499	Spinner Global Technology Fund, Caduceus Capital Ltd, America First Fin Institutions Invest
Sandler Offshore	2.68721	Sandler Offshore, Caduceus Capital Ltd, America First Fin Institutions Invest
KCM Biomedical	1.24732	KCM Biomedical, Caduceus Capital Ltd
Malta Hedge Fund II	2.06355	Malta Hedge Fund II, Keefe-Rainbow Partners, Financial Edge Fund
Acadia Fund	1.99535	Financial Edge Fund
Galleon Omni Technology Fund (A)	1.59817	Galleon Omni Technology Fund (A), Caduceus Capital Ltd, America First Fin Institutions Invest.

TABLE 8.8 *(Continued)*

Level 2 (CRS) DMU Name	Input-Oriented Level 3 (CRS) Context-Dependent Score	Benchmarks
Basswood Financial Partners	1.51196	Caduceus Capital Ltd, Financial Edge Fund, America First Fin Institutions Invest.
Caduceus Capital	1.04294	Caduceus Capital Ltd
Hangar 4 Eagle I	1.68967	Caduceus Capital Ltd, America First Fin Institutions Invest
Crestwood Capital Intl	1.36740	Caduceus Capital Ltd, America First Fin Institutions Invest
Polaris Prime Technology	1.37735	Caduceus Capital Ltd, Financial Edge Fund

TABLE 8.9 Long Only Using Context-Dependent DEA

Level 1 (CRS) DMU Name	Input-Oriented Level 2 (CRS) Context-Dependent Score	Benchmarks
Hamton I–Bond 004 {Euro}	1.19572	Marksman Partners
Rutledge Partners	1.28331	Marksman Partners

Level 1 (CRS) DMU Name	Input-Oriented Level 3 (CRS) Context-Dependent Score	Benchmarks
Hamton I–Bond 004 {Euro}	1.86304	Zazove Aggressive Growth Fund
Rutledge Partners	2.36090	KR Capital Partners Fund I, Zazove Aggressive Growth Fund

Level 2 (CRS) DMU Name	Input-Oriented Level 3 (CRS) Context-Dependent Score	Benchmarks
Marksman Partners	1.91617	KR Capital Partners Fund I, Zazove Aggressive Growth Fund

TABLE 8.10   Short Sellers Using Context-Dependent DEA

Level 1 (CRS) DMU Name	Input-Oriented Level 2 (CRS) Context-Dependent Score	Benchmarks
Permal Us Opportunities	44.11446	Arcas Intl Fund (Covered Interests)
C&O Investment Partnership	26.80669	Arcas Intl Fund (Covered Interests)

Level 1 (CRS) DMU Name	Input-Oriented Level 3 (CRS) Context-Dependent Score	Benchmarks
Permal Us Opportunities	163.30906	Arcas Covered Fund
C&O Investment Partnership	99.23673	Arcas Covered Fund

Level 2 (CRS) DMU Name	Input-Oriented Level 3 (CRS) Context-Dependent Score	Benchmarks
Arcas Intl Fund (Covered Interests)	3.70194	Arcas Covered Fund
Arcas Fund II (Covered Interests)	2.68855	Arcas Covered Fund

TABLE 8.11   Diversified CTA Using Context-Dependent DEA

Level 1 (CRS) DMU Name	Input-Oriented Level 2 (CRS) Context-Dependent Score	Benchmarks
Astmax Co (Genesis)	3.22008	Transtrend (Enhanced Risk USD)
Crabel Capital Mgt (Div Fut Unlev)	2.32269	Transtrend (Enhanced Risk USD)
Grinham Managed Funds Pty	1.28390	John W Henry & Co (Strat Allocation), Transtrend (Enhanced Risk USD), Campbell & Co (Gl/Diversified Large)
Beach Capital Mgt (Discretionary)	1.28778	Transtrend (Enhanced Risk USD)
Drury Capital (Diversified)	1.13197	Transtrend (Enhanced Risk USD), Winton Capital Mgt
Eckhardt Trading (Standard)	1.11894	Transtrend (Enhanced Risk USD)

TABLE 8.11 *(Continued)*

Level 1 (CRS) DMU Name	Input-Oriented Level 3 (CRS) Context-Dependent Score	Benchmarks
Astmax Co (Genesis)	3.45552	Rotella Capital (Standard Lev)
Crabel Capital Mgt (Div Fut Unlev)	3.05515	Rotella Capital (Standard Lev)
Grinham Managed Funds Pty	1.44300	Rotella Capital (Standard Lev), Millburn Ridgefield (Diversified)
Beach Capital Mgt (Discretionary)	1.58208	Rotella Capital (Standard Lev)
Drury Capital (Diversified)	1.35703	Rotella Capital (Standard Lev)
Eckhardt Trading (Standard)	1.41045	Rotella Capital (Standard Lev), Millburn Ridgefield (Diversified)

Level 2 (CRS) DMU Name	Input-Oriented Level 3 (CRS) Context-Dependent Score	Benchmarks
Sunrise Capital (Expanded Diversified)	1.10282	Rotella Capital (Standard Lev), Rabar Market Research
John W Henry & Co (Strat Allocation)	1.18369	Rotella Capital (Standard Lev), Millburn Ridgefield (Diversified), Rabar Market Research
Transtrend (Enhanced Risk USD)	1.46593	Rotella Capital (Standard Lev)
RG Niederhoffer Capital Mgt	1.15141	Rotella Capital (Standard Lev), Rabar Market Research
Winton Capital Mgt	1.21763	Rotella Capital (Standard Lev), Millburn Ridgefield (Diversified)
Campbell & Co (Gl/Diversified Large)	1.09506	Rotella Capital (Standard Lev), Millburn Ridgefield (Diversified), Rabar Market Research
Sunrise Capital (Diversified)	1.10930	Rotella Capital (Standard Lev), Rabar Market Research

TABLE 8.12 Financials CTA Using Context-Dependent DEA

Level 1 (CRS) DMU Name	Input-Oriented Level 2 (CRS) Context-Dependent Score	Benchmarks
John W Henry & Co (Fin & Metals)	1.24419	Eckhardt Trading (Global Financial), Marathon Capital (Financial)
Cornerstone Trading (Intl Value)	1.68764	Campbell & Co (Fin/Met/En Large), Eckhardt Trading (Global Financial)
Allied Irish Capital Mgt (Worldwide)	5.05364	IIU Breakout Program
Appleton Capital (Global Fin)	2.93437	Eckhardt Trading (Global Financial), IIU Breakout Program

Level 1 (CRS) DMU Name	Input-Oriented Level 3 (CRS) Context-Dependent Score	Benchmarks
John W Henry & Co (Fin & Metals)	1.59774	Capital Fund Mgt (Discus), Millburn Ridgefield (Global Financial)
Cornerstone Trading (Intl Value)	2.12457	Capital Fund Mgt (Discus), Campbell & Co (FME Small) Above $5M
Allied Irish Capital Mgt (Worldwide)	8.35801	Campbell & Co (FME Small) Above $5M
Appleton Capital (Global Fin)	5.84615	Campbell & Co (FME Small) Above $5M

Level 2 (CRS) DMU Name	Input-Oriented Level 3 (CRS) Context-Dependent Score	Benchmarks
Campbell & Co (Fin/Met/En Large)	1.20751	Campbell & Co (FME Small) Above $5M
Dunn Capital Mgt (WMA)	1.16959	Capital Fund Mgt (Discus), Millburn Ridgefield (Global Financial)
Dunn Capital Mgt (Tops)	1.23225	Capital Fund Mgt (Discus), Millburn Ridgefield (Global Financial)
Eckhardt Trading (Global Financial)	1.67619	Capital Fund Mgt (Discus), Millburn Ridgefield (Global Financial)
Marathon Capital (Financial)	1.37743	Capital Fund Mgt (Discus), Millburn Ridgefield (Global Financial), Campbell & Co (FME Small) Above 5M
IIU Breakout Program	2.00247	Campbell & Co (FME Small) Above $5M
Smith Point Invest (Regular)	1.09269	Campbell & Co (FME Small) Above $5M, Lyon Investment(Fin/Cur Contra Trend), Viguerie Investments

TABLE 8.13 Currency CTA Using Context-Dependent DEA

Level 1 (CRS) DMU Name	Input-Oriented Level 2 (CRS) Context-Dependent Score	Benchmarks
Allied Irish Capital Mgt (Forex)	2.39048	Analytic Investment Mgt (N-Lin), Hathersage Capital Mgt (Long-Term)
C-View Ltd	2.56570	Analytic Investment Mgt (N-Lin), Hathersage Capital Mgt (Long-Term)
Coral Rock Investment (White Coral)	3.20414	Analytic Investment Mgt (N-Lin)
Millburn Ridgefield (Currency)	1.09892	Sunrise Capital (Currency), John W Henry & Co (G-7 Currency)
Hathersage Capital (Daily Growth)	8.94687	Hathersage Capital Mgt (Long-Term), Compucom Finance

Level 1 (CRS) DMU Name	Input-Oriented Level 3 (CRS) Context-Dependent Score	Benchmarks
Allied Irish Capital Mgt (Forex)	4.90906	Ikos (Currency)
C-View Ltd	4.60492	Ikos (Currency)
Coral Rock Investment (White Coral)	7.03529	Appleton Capital (10% Risk)
Millburn Ridgefield (Currency)	1.22682	Willowbridge Associates (Currency)
Hathersage Capital (Daily Growth)	12.70409	Ikos (Currency), Willowbridge Associates (Currency)

Level 2 (CRS) DMU Name	Input-Oriented Level 3 (CRS) Context-Dependent Score	Benchmarks
Quantitative Financial (IPS Currency)	1.18929	Ikos (Currency), Jacobson Fund Managers (2.5X Lev)
Analytic Investment Mgt (N-Lin)	2.45417	Ikos (Currency), Appleton Capital (10% Risk)
Sunrise Capital (Currency)	1.26858	Ikos (Currency),Willowbridge Associates(Currency)
John W Henry & Co (G-7 Currency)	1.10848	Willowbridge Associates (Currency)
Jacobson Fund Managers (1.0X Lev)	1.67761	Ikos (Currency), Appleton Capital (10% Risk)
Hathersage Capital Mgt (Long-Term)	1.61172	Ikos (Currency)
Compucom Finance	1.57038	Ikos (Currency), Jacobson Fund Managers (2.5X Lev)
Marathon Capital (System FX)	1.21467	Ikos (Currency)

TABLE 8.14   Stock Index CTA Using Context-Dependent DEA

Level 1 (CRS) DMU Name	Input-Oriented Level 2 (CRS) Context-Dependent Score	Benchmarks
Analytic Investment Mgt (IFT)	1.35135	Witter & Lester (Intermediate)
Michael N Trading (FFTP)	2.13367	Oxeye Capital Mgt (Fut & Opt), Witter & Lester (Intermediate), Stan Udler (Global Index Program), Intl Trading Advisors (Index)
Strategic Investments (Equity Hedge)	1.19724	Stan Udler (Global Index Program), Intl Trading Advisors (Index)
Allied Irish Capital Mgt (Equity Index)	1.89047	Witter & Lester (Intermediate)
Witter & Lester (Redstone)	2.21469	Witter & Lester (Intermediate), Stan Udler (Global Index Program)

Level 1 (CRS) DMU Name	Input-Oriented Level 3 (CRS) Context-Dependent Score	Benchmarks
Analytic Investment Mgt (IFT)	2.99600	Witter & Lester (Stock Index)
Michael N Trading (FFTP)	5.99941	Ansbacher Investment Mgt
Strategic Investments (Equity Hedge)	2.29627	Ansbacher Investment Mgt, Witter & Lester (Stock Index)
Allied Irish Capital Mgt (Equity Index)	3.58019	Witter & Lester (Stock Index)
Witter & Lester (Redstone)	3.89928	Witter & Lester (Stock Index)

Level 2 (CRS) DMU Name	Input-Oriented Level 3 (CRS) Context-Dependent Score	Benchmarks
Oxeye Capital Mgt (Fut & Opt)	3.79589	Ansbacher Investment Mgt
Witter & Lester (Intermediate)	2.34373	Witter & Lester (Stock Index)
Stan Udler (Global Index Program)	3.21833	Ansbacher Investment Mgt
Intl Trading Advisors (Index)	2.84774	Ansbacher Investment Mgt

TABLE 8.15 Agricultural CTA Using Context-Dependent DEA

Level 1 (CRS) DMU Name	Input-Oriented Level 2 (CRS) Context-Dependent Score	Benchmarks
Strategic Investments (Agriculture)	1.51717	Range Wise

Level 1 (CRS) DMU Name	Input-Oriented Level 3 (CRS) Context-Dependent Score	Benchmarks
Strategic Investments (Agriculture)	2.35109	Yutaka Futures Co (Arbitrage)

Level 2 (CRS) DMU Name	Input-Oriented Level 3 (CRS) Context-Dependent Score	Benchmarks
Range Wise	1.56324	Yutaka Futures Co (Arbitrage), Agtech Trading Company

CONCLUSION

CDEA measures the attractiveness of hedge funds and CTAs within an evaluation context. Various efficient frontiers (as opposed to the standard first-level efficient frontier found in traditional DEA) are used as the evaluation contexts. In traditional DEA, deleting or adding an inefficient fund does not change the efficiencies of the funds or the efficient frontier. In context-dependent DEA, however, the performance of the efficient and inefficient funds are altered. In other words, CDEA does not rely solely on the efficient frontier. It also uses the inefficient hedge funds and CTAs, allowing DEA to recognize superior alternatives and offer more flexibility. The attractiveness measure can help investors and FOF managers identify hedge funds and CTAs that have achieved exceptional performance.

CDEA allows us to obtain more detailed information when comparing hedge funds and CTAs than would be possible via traditional DEA. CDEA recognizes the most attractive fund between the various levels of efficient frontiers, and also identifies the most attractive fund in terms of individual characteristics. This method can identify superior alternatives when a particular hedge fund and CTA are rated as inefficient by traditional DEA.

CHAPTER 9

Application of Fixed- and Variable-Benchmark Models

INTRODUCTION

This chapter uses benchmark models in Chapter 4 to compare efficiency among funds. Benchmarking models permit us to establish the relative standings of hedge funds and CTAs under investigation by ranking them in terms of efficiency.

Many types of performance measures used by investors can deal with only one measure at a time. DEA can examine numerous inputs and outputs simultaneously, and can be considered a benchmarking instrument because it uses the best practices frontier as the "gold" standard of efficiency. In this chapter, hedge funds and CTAs are appraised against a group of benchmarks (or standards).

By using a relative comparison approach with their peers, we obtain an efficiency score that ranks hedge funds and CTAs from the highest to the lowest. It is not uncommon for hedge fund managers or CTAs to try to rectify any inefficiencies by trying to follow the example of an efficient fund on the frontier in order to become efficient. The effectiveness of using benchmarking models in a DEA setting is an improvement over the use of traditional static market indices because of the dynamic strategies and non-normal returns that hedge funds and CTAs generate.

Many academic studies examining the performance of hedge funds and CTAs have used different benchmarks with little success. Using hedge fund indices as benchmarks when added to traditional stock and bond portfolios provides only partial information. This hurdle is overcome, however, when using fixed- and variable-benchmark models from DEA (Zhu, 2003), because the funds themselves are used as benchmarks. Selecting a subset of benchmarks is up to the discretion of the investors, FOF managers, or management.

For example, management may be interested in selecting benchmarks using another risk-adjusted measure such as the Treynor ratio. This ratio is a measure of risk-adjusted performance and is calculated by subtracting the risk-free rate from the portfolio's rate of return (that is, the excess return), and then dividing by beta to obtain the reward per each unit of risk. The greater the Treynor ratio, the better the fund's past risk-adjusted performance.

It is common knowledge that hedge fund managers and CTAs have control over the inputs they use. Therefore, in input-oriented fixed- and variable-benchmark models with constant returns-to-scale, a hedge fund manager or CTA is deemed inefficient if any input can be reduced without increasing any other input, and without reducing any other output (Zhu, 2003).

In the long-only, agricultural, and financials classifications, we only use one model, because the other results in solutions that are not feasible for some of the funds.

RESULTS

The Fixed-Benchmark Model (Input-Oriented)

We select the two funds with the highest Sharpe ratio from each classification and use them as fixed benchmarks (see Chapter 6). In Table 9.1, these are Edison Fund Class A and DKR International Relative Value (A). As we add more funds as fixed benchmarks, the performance of each hedge fund and CTA becomes worse, which makes it more difficult for funds to outperform both fixed benchmarks.

For a majority of classifications, we use both input-oriented variable returns-to-scale models. In our input-oriented fixed-benchmark model with variable returns-to-scale, a higher efficiency score indicates better performance. Using the variable returns-to-scale model, we assume the inputs of the funds do not generate a proportional change in outputs. Using the fixed-benchmark model in Table 9.1, Ironwood Partners attains the highest efficiency score (3.5972), while Man-Glenwood Multi-Strategy Fund yields the lowest (0.57104).

An FOF manager may be interested in observing how funds can outperform the "star" funds (benchmarks) by using various inputs and outputs. Some funds will have larger efficiency scores; others will be grouped around similar scores. This can give FOF managers another method for screening

TABLE 9.1 Fund of Hedge Funds Input-Oriented CRS-VRS Fixed- and Variable-Benchmark Scores

DMU Name	Input-Oriented VRS Fixed-Benchmark Score	Input-Oriented CRS Variable-Benchmark Score
GAM Diversity Fund	0.57299	0.51077
Permal Investment Holdings NV (A)	0.70170	0.58022
Haussman Holdings NV	0.74564	0.62552
Mesirow Alternative Strategies Fund	0.63541	0.74107
JP Morgan Multi-Strategy Fund	0.87291	0.82093
Man-Glenwood Multi-Strategy Fund	0.57104	0.56552
Coast Diversified Fund	0.97038	0.69691
Aurora	0.74468	0.76368
Lighthouse Diversified Fund	0.78044	0.75846
Mesirow Equity Opportunity Fund	0.81756	0.69107
Meridian Horizon Fund	0.77022	0.61096
Leveraged Capital Holdings	0.74200	0.77838
Ironwood Partners	3.59762	0.85474
Mesirow Event Strategies Fund	0.87367	0.60274
Momentum All-Weather Fund	0.58104	1.02154
Green Way Class B {Euro}	0.61051	0.80755
Permal Japan Holdings	1.24216	Benchmark
Asian Capital Holdings Fund	1.11017	Benchmark
Edison Fund Class A	Benchmark	Benchmark
DKR Intl Relative Value (A)	Benchmark	Benchmark

hedge fund managers or CTAs without the cumbersome use of hedge fund indices or static or long-only market indices.

In the fixed-benchmark model, a FOF, hedge fund, or CTA can select a subset of different benchmarks so that the performance of the new fund can be differentiated in the most positive aspect. In some cases, a category rated 100% efficient is not necessarily generating maximum outputs for the amount of inputs used, but it may be 100% efficient when compared to its peers. Because we use an input-oriented model with variable returns-to-scale for all hedge fund (Tables 9.1 through 9.10) and CTA classifications (Tables 9.11 through 9.15), funds with the highest scores have exceptional performance. The same analysis can be applied to the remaining classifications (Tables 9.2 through 9.15).

TABLE 9.2   Event Driven Input-Oriented VRS-CRS Fixed- and
Variable-Benchmark Scores

DMU Name	Input-Oriented VRS Fixed-Benchmark Score	Input-Oriented CRS Variable-Benchmark Score
Elliott Intl	0.66622	0.60420
Canyon Value Realization Cayman (A)	0.37463	0.42892
Elliott Associates	0.66887	0.64292
York Investment	0.88345	0.73069
Paulson Intl	0.62943	0.57098
Canyon Value Realization Cayman (B)	0.37984	0.42892
Canyon Value Realization Fund	0.42657	0.46373
Halcyon Offshore Event-Driven Strat	0.64841	0.63949
York Select	1.12152	0.72257
York Capital Mgt	0.87757	0.72667
Paulson Partners	0.61781	0.55924
Halcyon Fund	0.77693	0.73214
GAM Arbitrage	0.51397	0.51648
Gabelli Associates	0.68250	0.73989
Corsair Capital Partners (CCA)	0.87602	0.65649
American Durham	0.63522	0.61566
King Street Capital Ltd	1.04789	Benchmark
Triage Capital Mgt	0.98671	Benchmark
Caspian Capital Partners	Benchmark	Benchmark
King Street Capital	Benchmark	Benchmark

TABLE 9.3 Market Neutral Input-Oriented VRS-CRS Fixed- and Variable-Benchmark Scores

DMU Name	Input-Oriented VRS Fixed-Benchmark Score	Input-Oriented CRS Variable-Benchmark Score
Derivative Arbitrage Fund {Yen}	0.56990	0.45595
Ellington Composite	0.10378	0.50676
Shepherd Investments Intl	0.49756	0.74258
Stark Investments	0.51126	0.72500
III Fund Ltd	0.34961	0.67319
III Global	0.25320	0.48869
Ellington Overseas Partners	0.15487	0.43542
MBS Fund Gamma (O)	2.01962	3.41463
Alta Partners Ltd	3.00997	2.44771
Libertyview Plus Fund	0.54514	1.41949
Deephaven Market Neutral Fund	0.61804	0.92380
St Albans Partners	0.76995	1.27845
Mkt Neutral Equitized Strat Comp	0.45847	0.67770
Concordia Capital (A)	0.43571	1.46006
Argent Classic Conv ARB(Bermuda) (A)	0.50169	0.69876
Black Diamond	1.08018	2.06956
Deephaven Market Neutral Fund Ltd	0.64038	Benchmark
Double Black Diamond	0.76368	Benchmark
Millennium Intl	Benchmark	Benchmark
Alexandra Global Master Fund	Benchmark	Benchmark

TABLE 9.4 Global Macro Input-Oriented VRS Fixed- and Variable-Benchmark Scores

DMU Name	Input-Oriented VRS Fixed-Benchmark Score	Input-Oriented CRS Variable-Benchmark Score
Vega Global Fund	2.51177	2.08201
UBS Currency Portfolio	0.73360	0.77177
Global Undervalued Securities Fund	7.38832	1.36724
LCM GL Int Rate Hedged Fund (Opport)	0.77102	0.91010
CRG Partners LDC	0.86805	0.78728
Permal Europe {Euro}	0.75065	0.72490
Wexford Spectrum Fund	0.75207	0.76090
GAM Cross-Market	0.61937	0.83461
Grossman Currency Fund	0.84171	0.78035
Universal Bond Fund	0.61502	0.60322
Peak Partners	1.21987	Benchmark
Wexford Offshore Spectrum Fund	0.74657	Benchmark
Peak Partners	Benchmark	Benchmark
Global-Undervalued Securities Fund	Benchmark	Benchmark

TABLE 9.5 Global Emerging Input-Oriented VRS Fixed- and Variable-Benchmark Scores

DMU Name	Input-Oriented VRS Fixed-Benchmark Score	Input-Oriented CRS Variable-Benchmark Score
Ashmore Emerg Markets Liquid Invest	0.78780	0.78152
Hermitage Fund (Worst Bid)	0.76866	0.72614
Ashmore Local Currency Debt Port	1.19852	0.66987
GLS Offshore Global Opportunities	0.75491	0.74403
Firebird Republics Fund	0.65881	0.65659
Firebird New Russia Fund	0.74409	0.67222
EK Asia Fund	0.94201	0.92617
GLS Global Opportunities Fund	0.69850	0.68876
Griffin East European Value {Euro}	0.74342	0.74541
Tiedemann/Ayer Asian Growth	0.77591	0.75873
Key Global Emerging Markets	0.68815	0.67152
Firebird Fund	0.75722	0.74243
Ashmore Russian Debt Portfolio	1.25143	0.57721
Tradewinds Russia Partners I	0.85341	0.74918
Post Communist Opportunities Fund	0.81331	0.80647
Opportunity Fund Brazilian Hedge	1.13810	1.05718
Consulta Emerging Markets Debt	0.74865	Benchmark
Greylock Global Opportunity Fund	1.33701	Benchmark
Futurewatch	Benchmark	Benchmark
LIM Asia Arbitrage Fund	Benchmark	Benchmark

TABLE 9.6   Global Established Input- and Output-Oriented VRS Fixed- and Variable-Benchmark Scores

DMU Name	Input-Oriented VRS Fixed-Benchmark Score	Input-Oriented CRS Variable-Benchmark Score
BSteel Partners II	0.80656	0.95690
Adelphi Europe Fund (B) {Euro}	0.88656	1.04823
Odey European {Euro}	0.99978	0.91614
First Eagle Fund NV	0.67280	0.84436
Pegasus Fund {BP}	2.27185	1.18407
Libra Fund	0.68990	0.88960
Eagle Capital Partners	0.80461	0.94798
AJR International (A)	0.59295	0.86502
Amici Associates	0.96457	1.0570
Cambrian Fund (A)	0.54592	0.81496
Seminole Capital Partners	1.29422	1.39792
Everglades Partners	0.85684	0.87152
Giano Capital {Euro}	0.81073	0.92523
Adelphi Europe Fund (A)	0.87231	0.99291
Bricoleur Offshore	0.85022	0.85756
New Star Hedge Fund {BP}	0.79281	1.01195
Cobalt Offshore Fund	0.97816	Benchmark
Cobalt Partners	1.03474	Benchmark
Eureka Fund	Benchmark	Benchmark
Eureka Fund {Euro}	Benchmark	Benchmark

TABLE 9.7 Global International Input- and Output-Oriented VRS Fixed- and Variable-Benchmark Scores

DMU Name	Input-Oriented VRS Fixed-Benchmark Score	Input-Oriented CRS Variable-Benchmark Score
Orbis Global Equity	0.73937	0.83532
Orbis Leveraged {US}	0.89321	0.87038
Lazard Global Opportunities Ltd	0.62464	0.80945
Lazard Global Opportunities	0.67928	0.83786
GAM Selection	0.66002	0.79667
Equinox Partners	0.71342	0.83547
Glenrock Global Partners	0.55623	0.71545
Glenrock Global Partners (BVI)	0.54940	0.71277
Third Avenue Global Value Fund	0.72019	0.89615
Stewart Asian Holdings	0.93356	1.16907
Millburn Intl Stock Index Fund	0.59041	0.75419
Polaris Prime Europe	1.65461	1.47907
Zazove Global Convertible Fund	0.64858	0.82628
Aravis Clipper Fund	0.45467	0.64691
Performance Partners	1.28003	Benchmark
Orbis Optimal {US}	0.79707	Benchmark
Platinum Fund	Benchmark	Benchmark
IIU Convertible Fund	Benchmark	Benchmark

TABLE 9.8 Sector Input- and Output-Oriented VRS Fixed- and Variable Benchmark Scores

DMU Name	Input-Oriented VRS Fixed-Benchmark Score	Input-Oriented CRS Variable-Benchmark Score
Spinner Global Technology Fund	1.06415	1.23471
Basswood Financial Partners	0.85207	0.87356
Caduceus Capital Ltd	0.98454	1.30751
KCM Biomedical	0.88396	1.61523
Malta Hedge Fund II	1.05065	1.45723
FBR Ashton	0.90111	0.91138
Keefe-Rainbow Partners	0.75572	0.77335
Caduceus Capital	1.02606	1.31506
Dynamis Fund	0.93535	0.83657
Financial Stocks	0.74354	0.69541
Hangar 4 Eagle I	0.83542	1.47253
Financial Edge Fund	0.66768	0.80122
Crestwood Capital Intl	0.94322	1.07008
Digital Century Capital	0.88705	0.79249
Galleon Omni Technology Fund (A)	0.96005	1.58592
America First Fin Institutions Invest.	0.79897	0.81974
Polaris Prime Technology	0.91124	Benchmark
Sandler Offshore	1.11283	Benchmark
Sandler Associates	Benchmark	Benchmark
Acadia Fund	Benchmark	Benchmark

TABLE 9.9 Long Only Input- and Output-Oriented VRS Fixed- and Variable-Benchmark Scores

DMU Name	Input-Oriented CRS Variable-Benchmark Score
KR Capital Partners Fund I	0.69373
Rutledge Partners	1.52080
Marksman Partners	1.18506
Hamton I–Bond 004 {Euro}	Benchmark
Zazove Aggressive Growth Fund	Benchmark

TABLE 9.10   Short Sellers Input- and Output-Oriented VRS Fixed- and Variable-Benchmark Scores

DMU Name	Input-Oriented VRS Fixed-Benchmark Score	Input-Oriented CRS Variable-Benchmark Score
Arcas Intl Fund (Covered Interests)	0.72269	0.60846
Arcas Fund II (Covered Interests)	0.79453	0.62553
Arcas Covered Fund	1.41553	0.60369
Permal US Opportunities	Benchmark	Benchmark
C&O Investment Partnership	Benchmark	Benchmark

TABLE 9.11   Diversified CTA Input- and Output-Oriented VRS Fixed- and Variable-Benchmark Scores

DMU Name	Input-Oriented VRS Fixed-Benchmark Score	Input-Oriented CRS Variable-Benchmark Score
Astmax Co (Genesis)	0.98166	3.22008
Astmax Co (Prelude)	0.88043	0.90827
Crabel Capital Mgt (DIV FUT Unlev)	1.18789	2.32269
Rotella Capital (Standard Lev)	0.93210	0.98323
Grinham Managed Funds Pty	1.09585	1.26075
John W Henry & Co (Strat Allocation)	0.93768	1.06373
Graham Capital Mgt (GDP)	0.94921	0.96982
RG Niederhoffer Capital Mgt	0.82398	1.02457
Winton Capital Mgt	1.12809	1.02316
Millburn Ridgefield (Diversified)	0.85156	0.90966
First Quadrant (Managed Futures)	0.68034	0.83696
Campbell & Co (Gl/Diversified Large)	0.94692	1.01414
Rabar Market Research	0.84960	0.90482
Cipher Investment Mgt	0.96234	0.97943
Eckhardt Trading (Standard)	0.93372	1.10955
Sunrise Capital (Diversified)	0.96480	0.97806
Transtrend (Enhanced Risk USD)	1.02240	Benchmark
Sunrise Capital (Expanded Diversified)	0.99277	Benchmark
Beach Capital Mgt (Discretionary)	Benchmark	Benchmark
Drury Capital (Diversified)	Benchmark	Benchmark

TABLE 9.12   Financials CTA Input- and Output-Oriented VRS Fixed- and Variable-Benchmark Scores

DMU Name	Input-Oriented CRS Variable-Benchmark Score
Dunn Capital Mgt (WMA)	0.83226
Eclipse Capital (Global Monetary)	0.82785
Dunn Capital Mgt (Tops)	0.96369
Capital Fund Mgt (Discus)	0.96055
John W Henry & Co (Fin & Metals)	1.28560
Allied Irish Capital Mgt (Worldwide)	8.33753
Sunrise Capital (Financials-Cimco)	0.93324
John W Henry & Co (Global Fin & En)	0.83617
Marathon Capital (Financial)	1.05362
IIU Breakout Program	1.76900
Lyon Investment(Fin/Cur Contra Trend)	0.94731
Millburn Ridgefield (Global Financial)	0.88123
Smith Point Invest (Regular)	1.01570
Viguerie Investments	0.92811
Appleton Capital (Global Fin)	4.61552
Ashley Capital Mgt	0.87820
Cornerstone Trading (Intl Value)	Benchmark
Campbell & Co (Fin/Met/En Large)	Benchmark
Campbell & Co (FME Small) Above $5m	Benchmark
Eckhardt Trading (Global Financial)	Benchmark

TABLE 9.13   Currency CTA Input- and Output-Oriented VRS Fixed- and
Variable-Benchmark Scores

DMU Name	Input-Oriented VRS Fixed-Benchmark Score	Input-Oriented CRS Variable-Benchmark Score
FX Concepts (Developed Markets Cur)	0.87813	1.08167
Allied Irish Capital Mgt (Forex)	1.25073	1.26438
Ikos (Currency)	0.83283	1.03367
Analytic Investment Mgt (N-Lin)	0.65075	1.00431
Sunrise Capital (Currency)	0.90084	1.11494
John W Henry & Co (Intl FX)	0.90411	1.04839
Coral Rock Investment (White Coral)	1.86932	1.94138
Jacobson Fund Managers (2.5x Lev)	0.76294	0.81704
Appleton Capital (25% Risk)	0.94108	0.88017
John W Henry & Co (G-7 Currency)	1.16505	1.15906
Jacobson Fund Managers (1.0x Lev)	0.71488	0.83937
Compucom Finance	1.13537	0.98208
Appleton Capital (10% Risk)	0.76795	0.95370
Millburn Ridgefield (Currency)	1.06569	1.26392
Willowbridge Associates (Currency)	0.92364	1.14014
Marathon Capital (System FX)	0.88302	1.16064
Hathersage Capital (Daily Growth)	0.95599	Benchmark
C-View Ltd	0.80916	Benchmark
Quantitative Financial (IPS Currency)	Benchmark	Benchmark
Hathersage Capital Mgt (Long-Term)	Benchmark	Benchmark

TABLE 9.14 Stock Index CTA Input- and Output-Oriented VRS Fixed- and Variable-Benchmark Scores

DMU Name	Input-Oriented VRS Fixed-Benchmark Score	Input-Oriented CRS Variable-Benchmark Score
Ansbacher Investment Mgt	0.79762	0.80008
Analytic Investment Mgt (IFT)	0.60483	1.18528
Strategic Investments (Equity Hedge)	1.09698	1.20341
Witter & Lester (Intermediate)	0.69903	1.02528
Witter & Lester (Redstone)	0.54171	1.34959
Witter & Lester (Stock Index)	0.77308	0.91319
Intl Trading Advisors (Index)	1.00512	1.02090
Stan Udler (Global Index Program)	0.95188	Benchmark
Allied Irish Capital Mgt (Equity Index)	0.45689	Benchmark
Oxeye Capital Mgt (Fut & Opt)	Benchmark	Benchmark
Michael N Trading (FFTP)	Benchmark	Benchmark

TABLE 9.15 Agricultural CTA Input- and Output-Oriented VRS Fixed- and Variable-Benchmark Scores

DMU Name	Input-Oriented CRS Variable-Benchmark Score
Yutaka Futures Co (Arbitrage)	0.45507
Agtech Trading Company	0.58933
Kottke Associates (Crush)	0.44196
Strategic Investments (Agriculture)	Benchmark
Range Wise	Benchmark

The Variable-Benchmark Model (Input-Oriented)

In the variable-benchmark model (Zhu, 2003), we use the same two funds from the fixed-benchmark model, but also include two additional funds as benchmarks, which brings the total to four (Edison Fund Class A, DKR International Relative Value (A), Permal Japan Holdings, and Asian Capital Holdings). These funds are rated as the four highest using the Sharpe ratio (see Chapter 6).

Using the constant returns-to-scale model, we assume that any increase in the inputs of the funds will lead to a proportional increase in their outputs. For example, a 1% increase in standard deviation (input) will result in a 1% increase in compound return (output). The variable-benchmark model in Table 9.1 shows that the Momentum All-Weather Fund attains the highest efficiency score (1.02154); GAM Diversity attains the lowest. In Table 9.2, Gabelli Associates attains the highest efficiency score (0.73989), while Canyon Value Realization Cayman (A) and (B) are tied for last place with the lowest scores.

Hedge funds and CTAs attaining the highest scores can then be ranked in terms of efficiency from the highest to the lowest. Funds with the highest scores are on the best practices frontier, while funds with the lowest scores are above or below the frontier. So lower efficiency scores indicate that the FOF, hedge fund, or CTA is inefficient at producing results from its available resources on hand. In other words, an efficiency score of 0.8500 would indicate that the fund is actually 85% of the way to becoming efficient.

CONCLUSION

This chapter illustrates that fixed- and variable-benchmark models in a DEA setting are an alternative measure for ranking hedge funds, FOFs, and CTAs. Benchmarking provides insight because of the interaction of the benchmark with the hedge funds or CTAs. Using fixed- and variable-benchmark models can help institutional investors, FOF managers, pension funds, and high–net worth individuals select efficient hedge funds and CTAs without using traditional benchmarks. Of course, choosing funds by using the traditional benchmark criteria, such as the Sharpe, Treynor, or other ratios, may alter the rankings.

CHAPTER 10

Closing Remarks

We use different inputs and outputs to investigate the efficiency of hedge fund and CTA classifications. Because the selection of variables can affect efficiency scores as well as the rank order of hedge funds and CTAs, we strongly recommend that this technique be used as a complementary or alternative method to obtain further insight into the performance of hedge funds, funds of hedge funds, and CTAs.

Although DEA has been around for many years, it was first only applied to CTAs, FOFs, and hedge fund indices (Wilkens and Zhu, 2001; Gregoriou, 2003; Wilkens and Zhu, 2003. It was later applied to all hedge fund classifications (Gregoriou, Sedzro, and Zhu, 2005). A more recent paper by Gregoriou, Rouah, Satchell, and Diz (in press) investigated CTA classifications using basic and cross-efficiency DEA models using the Barclay data set. While historical data are useful, future research using longer time periods could prove even more valuable in comparing the efficiency of a greater number of hedge funds and CTAs.

We hope this book paves the way for such future research using various DEA models and expanded applications. Understanding how efficiency plays a role when hedge funds or CTAs endure bull or bear markets or extreme market events is of further interest. It would also be interesting to examine the efficiency of various hedge fund or CTA indices from various database vendors, or to investigate whether hedge funds or CTAs have greater efficiency persistence when using monthly, quarterly, or yearly data.

The DEA technique can be used in asset allocation, portfolio selection, financial planning, and many other applications. A family of hedge funds or CTAs can even investigate the efficiency of their individual funds by using proprietary information such as the number of staff, salary, portfolio turnover, and trading costs.

The growth of hedge funds has reached record levels over the last few years. There is no doubt that the DEA technique can add an important dimension to traditional regression analysis by making it possible to rate hedge fund managers, FOF managers, and CTAs on levels beyond performance. Hopefully, DEA will provide an increased level of confidence for both investors and fund managers to help them accurately assess the relative efficiency and quality of hedge fund and CTA management. For more information on DEA techniques, please refer to Zhu (2003).

References

Ackermann, C., McEnally, R., and Ravenscraft, D. (1999) The performance of hedge funds: risk, return and incentives. *The Journal of Finance*, 54(3), 833–874.

Agarwal, V., and Naik, N. Y. (2004) Characterizing hedge funds with buy-and-hold option based strategies. *The Review of Financial Studies*, 17(1), 63–98.

Anson, M. (2000) Selecting a hedge fund manager. *Journal of Wealth Management*, 3(3), 45–52.

Banker, R. D., Cooper, W. W., Seiford, L., Thrall, J., and Zhu, J. (2004) Returns to scale in different DEA models. *European Journal of Operations Research*, 154(2), 345–362.

Banker, R. D. and Thrall, J. (1992) Estimation of returns to scale using Data Envelopment Analysis. *European Journal of Operations Research*, 62(1), 74–84.

Barclay Trading Group (2003) Money under management in managed futures. http://www.barclaygrp.com/indices/cta/Money_Under_Management.html.

Brealey, R. A., and Kaplanis, E. (2001) Hedge funds and financial stability: an analysis of their factor exposures. *Journal of International Finance*, 4(1), 161–187.

Brown, S. J., and Goetzmann, W. N. (1997) Mutual fund styles. *Journal of Financial Economics*, 43(3), 373–399.

Brown, S. J., and Goetzmann, W. N. (2001) Hedge funds with style. *The Journal of Portfolio Management*, 29(2), 101–112.

Capocci, D. (2004) CTA performance, survivorship bias and dissolution frequencies. In *Commodity Trading Advisors: Risk, Performance Analysis and Selection*, Greg N. Gregoriou et al. (eds.) New York: Wiley, pp. 49–78.

Capocci, D., and Hubner, G. (2003) Analysis of hedge fund performance. *Journal of Empirical Finance*, 11(1), 55–89.

Charnes, A., Cooper, W. W., and Rhodes, E. (1978) Measuring the efficiency of decision-making units. *European Journal of Operational Research*, 2(6), 429–444.

Chatiras, M. (2004) The benefits of hedge funds: an update. Working paper, Centre for International Securities and Derivatives Markets (CISDM), University of Masschusetts, Amherst, MA.

Chicago Mercantile Exchange (1999) Managed futures account: a question and answer report. Chicago, IL.

Chicago Board of Trade (2003) *Managed futures portfolio diversification of opportunities*. Chicago, IL.

Cooper, W. W., Seiford, L., and Zhu, J. (2004) *Handbook on Data Envelopment Analysis*. New York: Kluwer.

Cvitanic, J., Lazrak, A., Martellini, L., and Zapatero, F. (2002) Optimal allocation to hedge funds: an empirical analysis. Working paper, University of Southern California, Los Angeles.

Edwards, F. R., and M. O. Caglayan. (2000) Hedge fund and commodity fund investment styles in bull and bear markets. *Journal of Portfolio Management*, 27(4), 97–108.

Edwards, F., and Caglayan, M. O. (2001) Hedge fund performance and manager skill. *Journal of Futures Markets*, 21(11), 1003–1028.

Fung, W., and Hsieh, D. A. (1997) Empirical characteristics of dynamic trading strategies: the case of hedge funds. *The Review of Financial Studies*, 10(2), 275–302.

Fung, W., and Hsieh, D. A. (1999) A primer on hedge funds. *Journal of Empirical Finance*, 6(3), 309–331.

Fung, W., and Hsieh, D. A. (2000) Performance characteristics of hedge funds and commodity funds: natural vs. spurious biases. *Journal of Financial and Quantitative Analysis*, 35(3), 291–307.

Gregoriou, G. N. (2002) Hedge fund survival lifetimes. *Journal of Asset Management*, 3(3), 237–252.

Gregoriou, G. N. (2003) Fund of hedge fund mortality. *Journal of Wealth Management*, 6(1), 42–53.

Gregoriou, G. N., Hubner, G., Papageorgiou, N., and Rouah, F. (2004) Survival of commodity trading advisors: 1990–2003. Working paper University of Liège, Belgium.

Gregoriou, G. N., and Rouah, F. (2004) Performance of the largest CTAs in negative S&P 500 months and extreme market events. *Journal of Wealth Management*, 7(1), 44–47.

Gregoriou, G. N., Rouah, F., Satchell, S., and Diz, F. (in press). Simple and cross efficiency of CTAs using data envelopment analysis, *European Journal of Finance*, forthcoming.

Gregoriou, G. N., Rouah, F., and Sedzro, K. (2002) On the market timing of hedge fund managers. *Journal of Wealth Management*, 5(1), 26–38.

Gregoriou, G. N., Sedzro, K., and Zhu, J. (2005) Hedge fund performance appraisal using Data Envelopment Analysis. *European Journal of Operational Research*, 164(2), 555–571.

Hubner, G., and Papageorgiou, N. (2004) The performance of CTAs in changing market conditions. In *Commodity Trading Advisors: Risk,*

Performance Analysis, and Selection, Greg N. Gregoriou et al. (eds.) New York: Wiley, pp. 105–128.

J. P. Morgan (September 20, 1994) *Internal report.* New York: NY.

Karavas, V. N. (2000) Alternative investments in the institutional portfolio. *Journal of Alternative Investments,* 3 (3), 11–26.

Kat, H. M. (2004) Managed futures and hedge funds: A match made in heaven. In *Commodity Trading Advisors: Risk, Performance Analysis, and Selection,* Greg N. Gregoriou et al. (eds.) New York: Wiley, pp. 5–17.

Kouwenberg, R. (2003) Do hedge funds add value to a passive portfolio? Correcting for non-normal returns and disappearing funds. *Journal of Asset Management,* 3(4), 361–383.

Liang, B. (2003) On the performance of alternative investments: CTAs, hedge funds, and funds-of-funds, Working paper, University of Massachusetts at Amherst.

Markowitz, H. M. (1952) Portfolio selection. *Journal of Finance,* 7(1), 77–91.

Markowitz, H. M. (1959) *Portfolio Selection: Efficient Diversification of Investments.* Cambridge, MA: Blackwell.

Martellini, L., and Vaissié, M. (2004) Benchmarking the performance of CTAs. In *Commodity Trading Advisors: Risk, Performance Analysis, and Selection,* Greg N. Gregoriou et al. (eds.) New York: Wiley, pp. 18–30.

Popova, I., Morton, D., and Popova, E. (2003) Optimal hedge fund allocation with asymmetric preferences and distributions. Working paper, Global Research Center, Deutsche Asset Management, New York.

Schneeweis, T. (June 22–25, 2003) Benefits of hedge funds/CTAs. Presentation to Investment Dealers Association of Canada (IDA) at the IDA 87th Annual Meeting and Conference, St. Andrews-by-the-Sea, New Brunswick.

Schneeweis, T., Spurgin, R., and Potter, M. (1996) Managed futures and hedge fund investment for downside equity risk management. *Derivatives Quarterly,* 3(1), 1–11.

Schneeweis, T., and Spurgin, R. (1998) Multifactor analysis of hedge funds, managed futures and mutual fund return and risk characteristics. *Journal of Alternative Investments,* 1(2), 1–24.

Schneeweis T., and Spurgin, R. T. (1997) Comparison of commodity and managed futures benchmark indices, *Journal of Derivatives,* 4(4), 33–50.

Schneeweis, T., Spurgin, R. T., and Georgiev, G. (2001) Benchmarking commodity trading advisor performance with a passive futures-based index, CISDM Working paper, University of Massachusetts, Amherst.

Seiford, L. M., and Zhu, J. (1999a) An investigation of returns to scale under data envelopment analysis. *Omega, International Journal of Mangement Science,* 27(1), 1–11.

Seiford, L. M., and Zhu, J. (1999b) Sensitivity and stability of the classification of returns to scale in data envelopment analysis. *Journal of Productivity Analysis*, 12(1), 55–75.

Seiford, L. M., and Zhu, J. (2003) Context-dependent data envelopment analysis: measuring attractiveness and progress. *Omega*, 31(5), 397–480.

Wander, B. (2003) Why skillful managers prefer equal-weighted benchmarks, *Journal of Wealth Management*, 5(3), 54–57.

Wilkens, K., and Zhu, J. (2001) Portfolio evaluation and benchmark selection: A mathematical programming approach. *Journal of Alternative Investments*, 4(1), 9–19.

Wilkens, K., and Zhu, J. (2003) Classifying hedge funds using data envelopment analysis. In *Hedge Funds: Strategies, Risk Assessment, and Returns*, Greg N. Gregoriou et al. (eds.) Washington: Beard, pp. 161–175.

Zhu, J. (1996) Data envelopment analysis with preference structure, *Journal of Operations Research Society*, 47(1), 136–150.

Zhu, J. (2003). *Quantitative Models for Performance Evaluation and Benchmarking*. Norwell, MA: Kluwer Academic Publishers.

Zhu, J., and Shen, Z. H. (1995) A discussion of testing DMUs returns to scale. *European Journal of Operational Research*, 81(3), 590–596.

Index

About the CD-ROM

Data Envelopment Analysis (DEA) is a relatively new "data oriented" approach for evaluating the performance of a set of peer entities called Decision Making Units (DMUs) which convert multiple inputs into multiple outputs. The definition of a DMU is generic and flexible. Recent years have seen a great variety of applications of DEA for use in evaluating the performances of many different kinds of entities engaged in many different activities in many different contexts in many different countries. These DEA applications have used DMUs of various forms to evaluate the performance of entities, such as hospitals, U.S. Air Force wings, universities, cities, courts, business firms, and others, including the performance of countries and regions. Because it requires very few assumptions, DEA has also opened up possibilities for use in cases which have been resistant to other approaches because of the complex (often unknown) nature of the relations between the multiple inputs and multiple outputs involved in DMUs. As *Evaluating Hedge Fund and CTA Performance* demonstrates, DEA is particularly useful in evaluating the efficiency of hedge funds, funds of funds, and commodity trading advisors (CTAs).

ABOUT DEAFrontier

DEAFrontier consists of a series of DEA softwares which are Add-Ins for Microsoft Excel developed by Joe Zhu. *DEAFrontier* uses Excel Solver, and does not set any limits on the number of DMUs, inputs or outputs. However, please check www.solver.com for problem sizes that various versions of Solver can handle. The standard Excel Solver shipped with Microsoft Office solves problems with sizes of 200 × 200. *DEAFrontier* software series require Excel 97 or later versions and Windows 95 or higher.

If you are using a non-English version of the Microsoft Office, the *DEAFrontier* software may not run properly.

DEAFrontier MICROSOFT EXCEL ADD-IN

The Excel Solver Parameters dialog box has to be displaced once before the *DEAFrontier* software is loaded. Otherwise, the *DEAFrontier* software may not run. (*If the* DEAFrontier *software is installed in the directory where the Excel Solver is installed, you may not need to load the Excel Solver first.*)

However, for some non-English versions of Microsoft Office, *DEAFrontier* software may still produce an error message if one attempts to use the DEA models. This may due to the fact that the "Solver.xla" is renamed in a local language in the Microsoft Office. For example, in some Finnish versions of Microsoft Office, "Solver.xla" is actually named as "ratkais.xla". In order to use the *DEAFrontier* software, one has to make sure that the Excel Solver is named as "Solver.xla" in its directory (usually Program Files\ Microsoft Office\Office 10\Library\Solver).

Please set the Macro Security to Medium Level in Excel. This can be done by selecting the Tools/Options menu item and click the Macro Security button and then select the "Medium" option.

If your Excel Solver file is named in your language, here is how to resolve the problem:

1. Make a copy of the *.xla file in its directory and rename its as "solver.xla".
2. Remove the non-English Excel Solver by unchecking the "Solver" add-in in your Excel Tools/Add-Ins window.
3. Install the renamed copy using Browse in Tools/Add-Ins window.

Alternatively, one can use the File/Open menu item to load the renamed Solver.xla manually from its directory. In this way, one does not have to "remove & install" as described above.

One can also run the Excel Solver from other directory. This is actually what one has to do if one uses the licensed premium solver platform or equivalent software. Therefore, if one does not want to change the original installation, one can create a new directory and copy all the Excel Solver related files into this new directory and then follow the above steps.

SYSTEM REQUIREMENTS

-   A computer with a processor running at 120 Mhz or faster
-   At least 32 MB of total RAM installed on your computer; for best performance, we recommend at least 64 MB
-   A CD-ROM drive

NOTE: *Many popular spreadsheet programs are capable of reading Microsoft Excel files. However, users should be aware that a slight amount of formatting might be lost when using a program other than Microsoft Excel.*

USING THE CD WITH WINDOWS

To install the items from the CD to your hard drive, follow these steps:

1. Insert the CD into your computer's CD-ROM drive.
2. The CD-ROM interface will appear. The interface provides a simple point-and-click way to explore the contents of the CD.

If the opening screen of the CD-ROM does not appear automatically, follow these steps to access the CD:

1. Click the Start button on the left end of the taskbar and then choose Run from the menu that pops up.
2. In the dialog box that appears, type d:\setup.exe. (If your CD-ROM drive is not drive d, fill in the appropriate letter in place of *d*.) This brings up the CD Interface described in the preceding set of steps.

WHAT'S ON THE CD

The following sections provide a summary of the software and other materials you'll find on the CD.

Content

The attached companion CD-ROM contains a powerful and fully functioning software called *DEAFrontier Basic*. The CD-ROM contains examples of data envelopment analysis (DEA) models in the book using live hedge funds and CTAs. This CD-ROM can benefit investors of all kinds in the selection of efficient hedge funds, funds of hedge funds, or CTAs. Readers can use other inputs and outputs at their discretion by simply creating similar spreadsheets as displayed in the examples and run the various models to obtain efficiency scores.

Included on the CD-ROM are the follow files:
Benchmarking.xls: An example file for Chapter 9
Context model.xls: An example file for Chapter 8
CTA.xls: An example file for Chapter 2
RTS.xls: An example file for Chapter 7
Solvertest.xls: An Excel file for testing the Excel Solver and is used in Chapter 2.
DEAFrontierbasic.xla: This file contains the main software program.

Customer Care

If you have trouble with the CD-ROM, please call the Wiley Product Technical Support phone number at (800) 762-2974. Outside the United States, call 1 (317) 572-3994. You can also contact Wiley Product Technical Support at http://www.wiley.com/techsupport. John Wiley & Sons will provide technical support only for installation and other general quality control items. For technical support on the applications themselves, consult the program's vendor or author.

To place additional orders or to request information about other Wiley products, please call (877) 762-2974.

ABOUT THE AUTHORS

Joe Zhu is an associate professor in the Department of Management at Worcester Polytechnic Institute. He is an expert in methods of performance measurement and his research interests are in the areas of productivity and performance evaluation and benchmarking. He has published two books focusing on performance evaluation and benchmarking using Data Envelopment Analysis (DEA) and has developed the *DEAFrontier* software. With more than 150 DEA models, this software can assist decision makers in benchmarking and analyzing complex operational efficiency issues in manufacturing organizations as well as evaluating processes in banking, retail, franchising, health care, e-business, public services, and many other industries. He has acted as consultant on efficiency and productivity issues. He is an associate editor of the *OMEGA* journal and a member of the Editorial Advising Board of Computers and Operations Research. Professor Zhu has published over 50 refereed papers in such journals as *Management Science, Operations Research, European Journal of Operational Research, Annals of Operations Research, IIE Transactions, Journal of Operational Research Society, Information Technology, OMEGA, Computers and Operations Research, INFOR,* and others.

Greg N. Gregoriou is assistant professor of finance and coordinator of faculty research in the School of Business and Economics at State University of New York (Plattsburgh). Greg received his Bachelor of Arts in Economics from Concordia University in 1988. In 1991, he completed his MBA and PhD (finance) from UQAM (University of Québec in Montréal). In addition to his university studies, Mr. Gregoriou has also completed several specialized courses from the Canadian Securities Institute and has published over 40 academic articles on hedge funds and commodity trading advisors in over a dozen peer-reviewed journals, such as the *Journal of Futures Markets, European Journal of Operational Research, Annals of Operations Research, Journal of Asset Management, Journal of Alternative Investments, European Journal of Finance, Journal of Financial Crime, Journal of Derivatives Accounting, Journal of Financial Services Marketing,* and *Journal of Wealth Management.* He is currently an associate with the Peritus Group in Montréal (www.peritus.ca). He is also the hedge fund editor and editorial board member for *Derivatives Use, Trading and Regulation,* a London, UK–based refereed journal–published by Henry Stewart. In May 2001, he was awarded the best paper prize in finance, with Fabrice Rouah, at the ASAC conference in London, Ontario. He has been invited to present his papers at numerous academic conferences. He is the coauthor and coeditor of three books on hedge funds and CTAs: *Performance Evaluation of Hedge Funds: A Quantitative Approach; Hedge Funds: Strategies, Risk Assessment, and Returns; and Commodity Trading Advisors: Risk, Performance Analysis, and Selection* published by John Wiley and Sons, Inc.

For more important information about the CD-ROM, see the About the CD-ROM section on page 163.